Laurence Olivier

W. A. Darlington

GREAT CONTEMPORARIES

Laurence Olivier

By W. A. Darlington

LAURENCE OLIVIER

Title page portraits.

Laurence Olivier as:

Iago in the 1938 Old Vic production of 'Othello'.

King Lear in the 1945/6 Old Vic production.

Coriolanus in the 1959 Stratford-upon-Avon production.

Astrov in the Chichester Festival/National Theatre production of Uncle Vanya.

GREAT CONTEMPORARIES
a division of
INTERNATIONAL PROFILES
General Editor: EDWARD STORER

English language editions published in:
GREAT BRITAIN, EUROPE and SOUTH AMERICA
by Morgan Grampian Books Limited,
28 Essex Street, Strand, London, W.C.2.

Series Design: Melvyn Gill.
Pictorial Research: F. G. Thomas.
Colour Plates: Photoprint Plates Ltd., Wickford, Essex and
W. S. Cowell, Ipswich, Suffolk.
Covers: George Over Limited, London and Rugby.
Paper: Frank Grunfeld (Sales) Limited, London.
Text: Photoprint Plates Ltd.
Printing and Binding: Hazell Watson and Viney Limited, Aylesbury
and London.

Introduction

1. *Laurence Olivier in the 1949 Old Vic production of 'Antigone'.* Angus McBean

First among the names of those whom I must thank for their help in the writing of this little book is that of my subject himself. My gratitude to Laurence Olivier is not for any practical assistance that he gave me, for I was careful not to ask him for any. During the whole of the time I was writing he was a desperately busy man, and during part of it he was under doctor's orders.

For me to have bothered him at such a time to supply me with facts or to verify conjectures was unthinkable and, in any case, unnecessary. The facts I needed were available from other sources, and much of what a critic has to say about an artist's work is, inevitably, conjectural. What I have to thank him for is that he gave the short work a blessing which he might understandably have withheld. I went to him, not to ask his permission to write about him, but to tell him that I had been invited to do so and had been delighted to accept. I knew that in thus presenting him with a *fait accompli* I was hardly going the best way about securing his goodwill, so I added the one plea which, I thought, might give me a claim on it. This was the happy accident (which I shall describe in its proper place in this book) that I had not only seen but noticed in the *Daily Telegraph* his first public performance when, as a schoolboy, he had played Katharina in *The Taming of the Shrew*. I had therefore not only followed his stage career from its very beginning but had, in a sense, helped to start him off on it. His response to this was warm and immediate. Of course it would be with all his best wishes that I should go ahead. Later, when the book was finished, he read it carefully in proof, made many helpful suggestions on small points, and in several important places enabled me to change conjecture into authenticated fact.

In the actual writing of the book, I am fortunate in having been able to supplement and solidify my own knowledge with that of various kind people in my circle of acquaintance who have encountered Olivier at one point or other of his career, and have not spared themselves in passing on to me what they knew of him.

Among these, my special thanks are due to Felix Barker, my fellow-critic, who in 1953 published *The Oliviers* (Hamish Hamilton), a very carefully compiled and well-documented account of the lives of Laurence Olivier and his second wife, Vivien Leigh, up to a point not very long before their spectacularly successful partnership came to grief.

Barker not only gave me a copy of his book, but made me free of the facts it contained. I have found those facts invaluable in building up the framework of my own narrative, and though I have checked them carefully I have found only one or two trifling inaccuracies in places where Barker's informant's memory has failed him and my own has happened to be more retentive. Where I have quoted direct from Barker's book I have acknowledged my source, but the full amount of my indebtedness to him is beyond assessment.

Another critical colleague to whom I owe thanks is my very old friend—J. C. Trewin. He gave me a copy of his book, *The Birmingham Repertory Theatre, 1913–1963* (Barrie and Rockliff), which contains a detailed account of Olivier's work for that theatre; and he kept me constantly supplied with any relevant facts which he thought might be useful to me. An account at first hand of

Olivier's early days as a professional actor was given me by Denys Blakelock, his closest friend of the time, who also gave me leave to quote from his autobiography *Round The Next Corner* (Gollancz).

Finally, I owe to two admirable and much-admired actresses vivid accounts of Olivier's remarkable performances as a young boy at the All Saints Choir School in Marylebone. Sybil Thorndike, already well on the way to fame, saw him in several of these performances and wrote me a glowing account of them, from which I shall quote. Fabia Drake, hardly older than Olivier but already a pupil at Tree's Academy, actually appeared with him in one of these productions—how heavily disguised, she lent me a much-prized photograph to show. It is reproduced on page 18.

2. *Laurence Olivier in the National Theatre production of 'Othello'.*   *Angus McBean*

Chapter I

3. Laurence Olivier during rehearsals at the National Theatre.   Dominic.

In 1962 the British National Theatre, for many years a dream and for many more a constantly-frustrated hope, became a living reality. Sir Laurence Olivier was made its first Artistic Director, and his appointment set the seal on a career of great distinction. It was a post which might have been given to an outstanding man of the theatre whose work lay in any of three fields—a manager, a stage-director, an actor. Olivier's claim was stronger than that of any possible rival because he had done notable work in all of these fields, and as an actor was generally acclaimed the brightest ornament the British stage had known since Irving.

The National Theatre was duly launched in its temporary home, the Old Vic, and very soon it became evident that its artistic director was exactly the right man in exactly the right place. From the first, Olivier set a very high standard in acting, production and design, and from the first it was clear that under his guidance there would be no danger that our National Theatre would become a dreary public institution, as some had feared. The response of playgoers was an almost embarrassing enthusiasm, and the only complaints came from disappointed people who had been beaten in the race for the cheaper seats and could not afford the dearer ones.

As the National Theatre's executive head, then, Olivier has earned himself already an honourable place in the history of our stage. Yet we have other men who could have done that part of his work equally well. It is as an actor that he stands unique and supreme, and therefore it is with his acting that I shall be chiefly concerned.

It was not until the National Theatre had been in existence for some six months that Olivier made his first important acting appearance on its stage, as Othello on 21st April, 1964. The occasion had been looked forward to with eagerness, but in the result it transcended expectations. The press notices were almost unanimously enthusiastic, and public response was immediate.

In the summer, the company moved to Chichester for a festival season, and a neighbour of mine in a Sussex village 50 miles away decided that this *Othello* was something which his two schoolgirl daughters must not be allowed to miss, and went to the telephone to book seats. A polite and regretful voice from the box-office said that every reserved seat for the remainder of the Festival had been booked. There were, of course, unreserved seats at each performance which could be obtained by waiting in a queue.

My neighbour thought this over. 'About what time,' he asked, 'should we have to begin waiting for seats at a *matinée*?'

'Round about noon . . .' (Come now, thought my neighbour, that's not so bad; but the box-office had not finished) '. . . the day before', it said.

That little anecdote, I suggest, sets forth more clearly than pages of laudatory prose the unique position that Laurence Olivier has won for himself in our theatre. The British people are both tough and patient when their interest is aroused, and will wait for great lengths of time in conditions of discomfort in order to be present at any event which they deem important. As a rule, however, fervour intense enough to cause such exhibitions of endurance is called forth only when vast crowds are involved and public feelings run high. Olivier's achievement is different in kind and in degree.

His was no appeal to the masses, but to that minority of the public who are playgoers. He was offering them the opportunity of seeing him on an unconventionally-designed, provincial stage, at an unpopular time of day, in a play centuries old and, at that, a tragedy. Another actor, even of the first rank, might well have failed to collect a full audience in such circumstances, but to see Olivier, people were willing to wait through a night and more than twice round the clock.

Nothing like that has happened in the theatre within living memory. Indeed, to find its counterpart we have to go back two hundred and odd years to the time when Garrick took the town by storm. Then, fine ladies wishing to secure tickets sent their footmen who arrived at dawn and lay sleeping on the ground to establish priority. Less wealthy citizens, who did their waiting in person, arranged breakfast-parties near the theatre so as to be on the spot when the scramble began. They had a shorter vigil to endure than Olivier's devotees at Chichester, but conditions were harder in the eighteenth century and crowds less orderly. All things considered, the two achievements are a fairly even match.

By common consent, Garrick is accounted the greatest actor the London theatre has ever had, and the fact that Olivier's name can be linked thus with his calls up at once the question how the greatest actor of our own time ranks for quality in company so exalted. That Olivier is the greatest actor we now have is an opinion so generally expressed, so firmly held in so many authoritative quarters, that it can be confidently accepted as a working hypothesis. There was a time when John Gielgud might have been thought pre-eminent, and if no other qualities were to be considered but subtlety of approach and beauty of delivery, he still might. But Olivier's power, his versatility and above all the virility of his attack have swept him to a supremacy now hardly ever doubted; and though our theatre can boast an array of actors of the first rank which can bear comparison with those of any time whatever, no single one of them can be named as Olivier's rival.

Accepting, then, that he has fairly won the right to be called by that grossly misused epithet 'great', and that he is the best we have, can we go on to claim for him a larger title still? The English theatre has never lacked for talent, and has a long and honourable list of 'great' players, men and women, who have served it; and among those names a few—a very few—have seemed to belong to beings of a separate race of giants. Garrick and Sarah Siddons, Edmund Kean and Irving have the air of being made of a different clay from their contemporaries, and to have had a power to move their audiences that was almost magical. The question faces us, is Laurence Olivier's name destined to rank with theirs?

It is a question (I realize, even as I ask it) that cannot be answered here and now; but the mere fact that the idea can be entertained in all seriousness is a mark of the actor's high stature. I feel, too, that posterity itself may have some difficulty in comparing an actor of today with the giants of the past. The last of those giants was Irving, and since the day when he let fall his robe to be picked up by the next comer big enough to wear it, the theatre has changed utterly; and, what is possibly more important, audiences have changed too.

In Irving's day the playhouse was a temple of the emotions. Audiences asked nothing better than to submit themselves to an actor's enchantment, to be made to laugh or cry at his will. Today, playgoers are better educated and less susceptible. They want to be allowed to think as well as be made to feel. The actor has had to change his methods to meet this new demand, and the result may be seen in the difference between Olivier's Othello and one or two very fine performances of the part seen in London almost half a century earlier.

Such actors as Godfrey Tearle or Matheson Lang, for instance, would see Othello as a dignified Arab, whose self-control was shaken but never wholly lost under Iago's evil influence. They would rely for emotional effect upon Shakespeare's great speeches; and I can still remember the beauty of Tearle's voice as he delivered them, and how moved I was by it. Olivier's Othello, on the other hand, was an uninhibited Negro, whose aim was not so

8

much to cause emotion in his audience as to exhibit it in himself. There never has been, I suppose, a more complete impersonation of a black man by a white one. The actor seemed to have transformed himself, to have altered the way his very joints were put together. It was a magnificent performance, but it was only very doubtfully Shakespeare's Othello. Some of Shakespeare's finest poetry was spoken at top speed in a high scream and was, as poetry, completely lost. I found myself greatly excited by the extraordinary display, but of pity I felt hardly a trace.

To the strictly orthodox lover of Shakespeare, then, Olivier's Othello was not likely to have any very full appeal; but to the contemporary generation of playgoers, trained as they were to see Shakespeare's plays subjected to every kind of experiment, it seemed something near to perfection. At the Old Vic, it became the most sought-after performance that the National Theatre has yet staged, and was kept in the repertory for a long time. Even when two years had gone by, complaints were still being made by frustrated playgoers that it was not being staged often enough. Olivier's answer to that was that only under repertory conditions could he have continued to stage it at all. The day after each performance, he said, he felt as though he had been run over by a bus, and to play the part twice consecutively would be altogether beyond his strength. This proves once again, if ever it needed proof, that the essence of a great actor is that he has reserves of energy and vitality denied to ordinary men, and that he gives a great performance when he is able to spend those reserves utterly.

In any attempt to state Olivier's right to assume the giant's robe then, special regard must be paid to the character of his audiences. The old race of giants were spell-binders who could exercise what seems to have been something very like hypnotic control over large groups of people, and the playgoers of their time seem to have yielded to their enchantments without a struggle.

This was not strange so far as the cheaper parts of the theatre were concerned, for the unsophisticated and uneducated mob which filled them was easily moved to mass hysteria. What does need explanation is the fact that people who were both highly educated and deeply sophisticated were almost equally at the mercy of strongly emotional acting. The German observer

Lichtenberg wrote of Garrick's audience with respect as being the best in Europe; yet it is on record that Garrick once brought down the house in a poor, long-forgotten play by the force with which he spoke the two banal words 'Thou traitor!' Mrs. Siddons once spoke a cue-line with such power that Charles Mayne Young's throat dried up and he could not speak his line at all. Edmund Kean's Shylock drove his first Drury Lane audience into paroxysms. Irving could bring a whole audience to its feet without anybody knowing how it had happened.

The eighteenth century prided itself on its sensibility, and gave way to its emotions without shame. The nineteenth, though engaged in cultivating the stiff upper lip, was deeply sentimental. Neither had any real defence against the spell-binders. The twentieth-century audiences before whom Olivier appears have little in common with their predecessors. Toughened and disillusioned by two world wars, accustomed to taking scientific miracles in their stride, and with their more impressionable elements drawn off by cinema and television, they are a formidable body, suspicious of romance, terrified of being betrayed into sentimentality, and therefore determinedly cynical. One can imagine them contemptuously impervious to the magic of a Siddons or an Irving; but I believe that they would find their resistance crumbling before a resurrected Garrick or Edmund Kean, both of whom were hailed in their day as pre-eminently 'natural' actors, and both of whom might therefore have been able to adapt themselves to the much more natural style demanded of actors today.

There are several ways in which Olivier can be said to be the same *kind* of actor as Garrick. Apart from 'naturalness', which in this connexion means freshness of outlook rather than realistic style, qualities common to both are versatility and love of disguise. Against Garrick's enormous range, from King Lear to Abel Drugger, may be set Olivier's, from Oedipus or Othello to Justice Shallow or Archie Rice. Kean was not especially versatile; comparison with him lies in directness of attack.

None of the three were (or are) particularly outstanding as heroes of romance. Garrick's Romeo was generally thought inferior to Spranger Barry's. Kean's great strength lay in parts like Shylock, Sir Giles Overreach (a part which nobody else seems able to play at all) or Richard III. Olivier, too, has acted a fine Richard III, the best I remember having seen, and others of his Shakespearean *tours de force* have been Macbeth and Coriolanus.

His Romeo was exciting, because it was played with such passionate vigour that throughout the balcony scene the possibility never seemed remote that he might swarm up a pillar and cut the play short by an act or two by having his desire there and then instead of hanging about in the garden talking imperishable verse. This must have been exciting for Juliet as well as for the audience—indeed, his Juliet on this occasion, Peggy Ashcroft, has said that it was—but it cannot have been quite what Shakespeare intended, and there was little about it of the decoration of romance.

So far, then, as range and intention go, the comparison between Olivier and the greatest of his predecessors is clearly valid. So far as such other essential qualities as concentration and dedication are concerned, this short account of his career will show that the comparison still holds. Whether he is to be accounted their equal, or close competitor, in power and stature is something which must be left to the judgement of the historians.

4. *Laurence Olivier with Joyce Redman in the 1945 production of 'Richard III'.*   John Vickers

Chapter 2

Radio Times Hulton Picture Library

5. Laurence Olivier in his first stage appearance as Katherine in 'The Taming of the Shrew'.

There is a widely-held belief that acting talent is hereditary, and the existence of families like the Kembles, the Keans, the Irvings, the Terrys, the Redgraves, or the Lupinos certainly makes the theory sound plausible. An alternative theory, however, might well be that such families have environment and example to thank, at least as much as heredity, for the ease with which they take to the stage. The world of the theatre is proverbially a world apart, having its own laws and customs and values. Those who are born into that world accept it from childhood.

If you are destined to be a great actor or actress, your best plan is to get yourself born into a theatrical family, as did Sarah Siddons or Eleonora Duse. That way you grow up taking for granted the laws and customs and values of the theatre world. You see your parents and relations living a backstage life and giving perform-ances in public, you realize that in due course you may do this too and from the start you know how.

Failing that, you can hardly do better than be born, as Laurence Olivier was, into a family of clergymen. Here, too, you grow accustomed to the sight and sound of your elders, clad in garments of ceremony, laying siege in public to the emotions and intellects of groups of rapt spectators, and you look forward to the day when you too will behave in much the same spectacular way.

It would not be easy to imagine a more firmly established family tradition than that of the Oliviers for taking holy orders. Huguenot in origin, they brought their stern Protestantism to England in the seventeenth century, and settled down to the production, generation by generation, of a phalanx of Anglican parsons. Except for a backslider who became a successful diamond merchant and left the family better endowed than he found it, there were few who did not conform, at any rate in the direct descent.

Laurence Olivier's father, Gerard Kerr Olivier, was himself a clergyman and a clergyman's son, but in him the Church tradition gave signs of petering out. Taken to Italy by his parents in his youth he was discovered to have a fine singing voice, and a noted Italian teacher offered to train him for opera. This excited his ambition; but his mother, deeply shocked, told him that if he adopted 'that monstrous profession' he would be cut off with a lira, and the impulse subsided. Later on, at Oxford, he lost his faith and came down without a degree. There was a story that the authorities sent him down for some wild exploit, but the evidence for this seems doubtful. At all events, he finished his education at Durham University and became a schoolmaster.

In his middle thirties, however, having scraped together enough money to start a school of his own, he complicated his own life and those of his wife and young family (a girl and two boys of whom Laurence was the youngest) by being reconverted to Christianity, selling the school, and taking orders. With a convert's enthusiasm, he now developed extremely High Church views and a strong taste for ritual which made him unacceptable to all but a few congregations.

As a result, for some years the family lived like nomads while its head, Father Olivier as he now liked to be styled, took temporary job after temporary job, sometimes acting as *locum tenens* while the regular incumbents took their holidays. The effect on his younger son, who seems to have been at that time a shy and withdrawn little boy, was that he was never given time to make friends outside his own family and was left very much to amuse himself.

This he did without any difficulty at all. Father Olivier was a dramatic preacher, and one of his young son's favourite games was to conduct services before a toy altar. Another game was play-acting. On a makeshift stage he would sing or dance or act for hours together, whether with the help of his elder brother, Dickie, or by himself, it made little difference. What, precisely, he was acting is not now known; mainly it was improvised on the spot and forgotten almost at once.

In 1912, when Laurence was five—he had been born at Dorking on 22nd May, 1907—there came at last a period of stability. Father Olivier was given the post of assistant priest at St. Saviour's, Pimlico, and the family moved into 22 Lupus Street, where they had a settled home at last and were to continue to live for the next six years, until a move was made at the end of the war when Father Olivier accepted a living at Letchworth Garden City.

Seldom can a boy's childhood games of make-believe have pointed forward more clearly to a choice that must later be made between two professions, but the question whether he would follow his father into the Church or strike out a line of his own on the stage hardly seems to have occurred to him at this time. Probably he assumed, as a young boy easily assumes, that he would go the way along which so many of his ancestors had gone—the more so because he was himself at this time deeply religious, taking his colour from his environment.

Without his knowledge, however, the question both posed itself and answered itself; and by an ironic twist of fate, it was the very step forward which seemed most likely to take him into the Church that turned him in the end away from it.

Not much of the diamond merchant's wealth had ever come Father Olivier's way, and the problem of how to give his two sons a good education was a difficult one; but it was solved by a stroke of fortune. Both boys were given places in the small choir school, limited to 14 boys, attached to the Church of All Saints, Margaret

Street, in Marylebone; and it chanced that the Precentor of that church, Father Geoffrey Heald, was one of those schoolmasters with a genius for persuading boys to act. Such men are not particularly rare—I have known half a dozen of them and have heard of many others—but the results they can conjure out of their pupils, especially the younger boys for whom the self-consciousness that develops with puberty is not yet a barrier, can be astonishing.

Father Heald was accustomed to turning out excellent and moving performances, but he very soon found that in the younger of the Olivier brothers he had a recruit who needed no coaxing and very little coaching—a natural actor of enormous vitality and enthusiasm. Cast as First Citizen in a production of *Julius Caesar* the nine-year-old Laurence showed such promise that he was promoted to play Brutus.

It chanced that the Pimlico parish where Father Olivier worked marched with another of which Canon Arthur Thorndike had charge. The Canon's daughter, Sybil, on the brink of making her name as an actress of the very first rank, was a friend of the Oliviers, who asked her and her husband, Lewis Casson, to go and see the *Julius Caesar* production.

Here let Dame Sybil herself take up the tale: 'We were astonished at Larry's skill,' she writes. 'It was quite wonderful. We came home to Gerard and said: "You can't keep that boy off the stage, he's a born actor." He had what we call "address"—he *used* his audience, as he does now. And that extraordinary vitality was evident, even at that age. We saw him play Sir Toby Belch* another time, also Katharina the Shrew. He was the best Katharina I've ever seen!—a real shrew but *very* touching. In all these three parts he showed the true instinct of the actor. It was not a child's performance—he was born with technique.'

In corroboration of that last remark may be added Ellen

---

*Either Dame Sybil's magnificent memory has, for once, played her false, or her equally excellent eyes were deceived at the time. Laurence Olivier played Maria in this production of *Twelfth Night*. It was the actress, Fabia Drake, then as a young girl a member of the All Saints congregation, but already a pupil at Tree's Academy, who smothered herself in a beard and played Sir Toby. In an anonymous cast otherwise consisting of boys with unbroken voices, her disguise was complete. See photograph on page 18.

Terry's observation after seeing *Julius Caesar*—'The small boy who played Brutus is already a great actor.'

How far Laurence Olivier himself was aware of, or joined in, the excitement he was causing his elders, there is little evidence to show. His father's aloofness and his own self-absorbed shyness prevented any very close contact at this time; and, indeed, various descriptions combine to give the impression of a rather forbidding young creature with whom no-one would lightly meddle. In the letter already quoted Sybil Thorndike says, in a tone of affectionate amusement: 'Such a fierce little fellow he looked—fiery, almost savage', and Denys Blakelock, who as a young actor had his first glimpse of his future friend as Katharina at All Saints, says in his own autobiography: 'He (Olivier) was not good-looking as a boy; he had a rather dark, glowering look, which was admirably suited to the Shrew.' This air must have been made to seem even more truculent still by a pair of heavy eyebrows and a mass of unruly hair growing very low on his forehead.

At any rate it did not look as though Gerard Olivier, in arranging for the next step in his son's education, had taken much notice of the Cassons' verdict that he would not be able to keep that boy off the stage. The choice was his alone, for his wife had died suddenly in 1920, and he picked St. Edward's, Oxford, as a suitable school for a prospective ordinand, and one which took the sons of clergymen at a reduced fee. To that school Laurence went in the September term of 1921.

Today, Sir Laurence Olivier is one of the school's most proudly acclaimed Old Boys, but during his time there he made no mark and was unhappy. He was moody, sometimes sullen and morose, sometimes wildly over-excited. (Geoffrey Heald had once described him to Denys Blakelock as 'a great bouncing St. Bernard puppy'.) Also he had not yet learnt the art of making friends. Moreover, he was 'pi', and that is no recommendation among schoolboys, even if a number of them are going to be parsons. He was unpopular, and well aware of it. Felix Barker quotes an extract from Olivier's diary after the school play at Christmas, 1923: 'Played Puck very well—much to everybody's disgust.' His vitality was, however, remarked upon by an amateur critic in the school magazine who wrote that he had more 'go' than any of the others.

But although he did not allow anybody at St. Edward's to

know it, Laurence had already by that time made his debut on the public stage and had had his first press notices.

Father Heald's production of *The Taming of the Shrew* had excited so much comment among the many stage people who worshipped at this fashionable church that the governors of the Memorial Theatre at Stratford-upon-Avon had invited him to stage the All Saints production in their theatre during the Birthday Festival of 1922. As this fell during the school holidays, Heald had been able not only to accept the engagement but to invite his original Katharina to repeat her former success.

That special matinée was noticed next morning by the 'special correspondent' of the *Daily Telegraph,* which then followed the ancient custom of anonymous criticism. That special correspondent was in fact myself; but because the schoolboy cast was also anonymous, I did not realize till many years afterwards that the boy whose image as the Shrew had stuck so firmly in my memory had been Olivier. With much misgiving I looked up the files of the *Telegraph* to see if I had paid due tribute to his early promise, and read with relief what I had written: 'The boy who took the part of Kate made a fine, bold, black-eyed hussy, badly in need of taming, and I cannot remember any actress in the part who looked better.'

This, I venture across the years to hope, may have encouraged him to find his vocation, and so may a notice in *The Times* which said that his performance did not call for patronizing indulgence; it had fire of its own. Yet he seems to have been still content to let events take their course, until a day came in January 1924, when he and his father at last came to understand one another.

The occasion was the departure of his elder brother to a plantation in India. Reacting to a sudden sense of loss, Laurence told his father that he would like to join Dickie in India when he left school. He received the crisp and, to him, utterly astonishing answer: 'Don't be a fool—you're going on the stage.'

Chapter 3

By courtesy of Miss Fabia Drake.

6. The Choristers of All Saints in their production of 'Twelfth Night' with Laurence Olivier as Maria and Fabia Drake as Sir Toby Belch.

Before he had absorbed the shock of this announcement, Laurence had to face another surprise. He found that the parent whom he had thought uninterested in his future had in fact given a good deal of thought to it, and that plans for his approach to the stage had already been roughed out. These plans were discussed and agreed in a long talk between father and son that evening.

It was settled that Laurence should leave St. Edward's at the end of the summer term and become a pupil of Elsie Fogerty's in the autumn. Miss Fogerty was very much a personality in the theatre of those days. She had founded and was principal of the Central School of Speech Training and Dramatic Art, which after her day removed to Hampstead but which at this time was curiously and not very comfortably housed in the upper regions of the Albert Hall. She was an uncompromising Irishwoman, rather formidable on first acquaintance but with a rough charm all her own. She had a genius for speech-training, by which not only the pupils in her school, but established actors and actresses—Sybil Thorndike among the number—were able to benefit. Laurence's elder sister had had a course at the school, and there seemed to be a chance that, if his promise appealed to her, Elsie Fogerty might be ready to ease his way with a grant or a scholarship.

In the event she did better for him than he had dared to hope. Her school was suffering from a desperate dearth of males (it is a regular disease of drama schools to be short of men and silted up with girls) and she not only gave him a scholarship which consisted of a year's tuition, but added a bursary of £50 to help towards his living expenses.

His year at the Central School was certainly not a failure, but it was not the unqualified success which must have been hoped for by those who had seen him as a child. One of his teachers, Henry Oscar, was able to see very little sign of talent in his work, and was subsequently to account for this by the belief that Olivier, only 17 at the time, was inhibited by the self-consciousness of adolescence and had lost for the time being his characteristic vitality. Oscar was a good actor, an experienced teacher, and a shrewd man, and his judgement in this case may well have been right. It is a fact well known to those who handle drama in secondary schools that many boys who at 13 or so have given remarkable performances cannot act at all once the age of puberty is reached.

At least Olivier was not one of these. Some of his lost talent soon struggled back, and at the end of his first term, when Athene Seyler judged the performances in the *Merchant of Venice*, there was some quality about his very hirsute Shylock that made her bracket him for top marks with the best of the girls, Peggy Ashcroft. And in his second term, with nothing much to beat, he took the Dawson Milward cup for the best of the men. The girls' cup was won by Peggy Ashcroft, so once again their names were coupled. These exploits, gratifying enough in themselves, were of purely local significance—as he was to find when he began to haunt the agents' offices in search of jobs.

During his time at the School he made a gallant attempt to live on his bursary money, taking a minute room in Castellain

Road, Paddington. The journey to and from Letchworth was too long to be made daily, and besides that an event had taken place which made him unwilling to live at the rectory. His father, who in theory believed that an Anglo-Catholic priest should be celibate, had married again. Laurence liked his step-mother, but his own strong Anglo-Catholicism made him disapprove of her existence as such. It was some little time before he became reconciled to the situation.

Meanwhile he almost starved. It was not really possible for a hungry boy of 17 or 18 to live in London in the mid-1920's on less than a pound a week; and though it was possible for a pupil in an accredited drama school to get work of a sort during the holidays, and though he did get his share of what was going in the way of small parts and (more often) assisting stage managers, none of it amounted to a living wage.

When his time at the Central School ended with the summer term of 1925 and his bursary no longer gave its useful support he found himself for a while quite desperately poor. He had accepted a minute allowance of £1 a month from his father, but he had to live as best he could without a job until October brought an engagement with the Lena Ashwell Players; and he contrived to lose that by giving way to an untimely fit of the giggles on stage when playing Flavius in *Julius Caesar*. However, it was noticed at All Saints that he was looking thin and undernourished, and this may have been the reason why, just before Christmas, he was offered £3 a week to walk on, and understudy if required, in Lewis Casson's production of *King Henry VIII* at the Empire. It afterwards became Sybil Thorndike's boast that her train as Queen Katharine in that production had been carried by two future knights, the film director Carol Reed being the other. This tided him over for a space, but it was not until the following year, 1926, that he got his real start.

This was unspectacular enough. Barry Jackson, a man of assured wealth with a passion for the theatre, had established himself in Birmingham with the famous little Repertory Theatre which he had built and managed, and was now casting an ambitious eye on London. Olivier went to an audition at the Kingsway Theatre, hoping for the name-part in *The Marvellous History of Saint Bernard,* Jackson's own version of a French mystery play.

He did not get the part, which was given to a more experienced actor, Robert Harris; but he was invited to understudy Harris and play a small part. In the event, he had to be content with a position more lowly still. Denys Blakelock became the understudy, and the rather resentful Olivier found himself with the not very impressive appointment of second understudy.

The play ran for two months, when it had to be taken off owing to the General Strike; but Olivier's work had impressed Barry Jackson enough for him to be kept on as a member of the company at Birmingham.

Here he was to stay for two years, possibly the two most important years of his life. It was during this time that he found himself developing away from the rather feckless boy, at times remote and forbidding and at other times excitable and over-demonstrative, that he had previously been.

Here he learnt to put down roots, to make friends, to show what he was made of. And above all, here he learnt to present himself as an actor not merely determined to make his way, but with a clear idea how to do so.

The chief authority on Olivier at this most formative point in his career is Denys Blakelock who was his closest friend—indeed, his first really close friend—at this time, and who devotes a chapter of his autobiography to a warm and detailed description of this friendship. It began with their association in the *Saint Bernard* play, in which Blakelock, besides being first understudy to Robert Harris, was playing the Archangel Gabriel. Six years older than Olivier, he was already an established London actor; they did not therefore act together once the *Saint Bernard* play was off, but they had so much in common that by that time a life-long relationship had been established.

Both were devout Anglo-Catholics, sons of Anglo-Catholic clergymen. It was as a member of that community that Blakelock had been invited in 1922 to be present at the performance of *The Taming of the Shrew* at All Saints, and had been so deeply impressed by Olivier's performance as Katharina. They had not met at that time, but at the Kingsway Olivier's self-introduction 'I think you know Father Heald' acted as an 'open sesame' of real power.

According to Blakelock, they talked endlessly on the two

subjects that woke their enthusiasm—religion and the theatre—and very little about anything else.

Olivier was always welcome in Blakelock's father's London vicarage, and Blakelock in his turn used to go often to the pretty little village of Addington, in Buckinghamshire, where Father Olivier had found his last parish. The elder of the two friends had plenty of opportunity to watch and admire the steady progress of the younger.

At Birmingham, Olivier found his feet. His tendency to wild bursts of irresponsible behaviour, due to his superabundant vitality, nearly got him into bad trouble, but he survived this, and gradually turned himself into a valuable, and valued, member of the company. At Birmingham too, he met for the first time with Ralph Richardson who was to become his life-long friend and constant partner.

This friendship began badly. At their first meeting the two men felt an intense mutual dislike. Richardson, some years the elder, thought Olivier frivolous and immature; Olivier found Richardson chillingly superior. Also, in the background, was the awkward fact that Olivier, who was constantly conceiving romantic attachments for the young actresses of the company, was at the moment in love with Richardson's charming young wife, Muriel Hewitt. This situation soon resolved itself, however; and perhaps the friendship was all the more solid for not having been too casually begun.

In 1926, when Olivier joined the Birmingham Repertory Theatre, Barry Jackson was still enjoying his greatest success, that of Eden Phillpotts's *The Farmer's Wife*, and it was with one of the touring companies of this play that Olivier had his first taste of steady employment. He must have done well with his part as a love-sick young farmer, for on his arrival back in Birmingham itself in December he was taken on as juvenile lead for the second half of the winter season. At once his reputation began to grow and his versatility to assert itself. He played parts as utterly different as Tony Lumpkin and Uncle Vanya, and was the Parolles in a modern-dress production of *All's Well that Ends Well* which excited the amused admiration of Bernard Shaw, for whom this play had a particular fascination.

At the beginning of his second Birmingham season Olivier was given the part of the young squire in John Drinkwater's country comedy *Bird in Hand*. A point of special interest to him was that the part of the innkeeper's daughter with whom the young man had fallen in love was played by his fellow-pupil at the Central School, Peggy Ashcroft. Both won praise, but the play itself, destined later to have a long London run and to restore Drinkwater's reputation as a dramatist, made no particular stir.

He was less lucky in Elmer Rice's *The Adding Machine* in which he had only a small part; but he played that small part well enough to be asked to play it again when Barry Jackson took a lease of the Court Theatre and moved the play up to London, and well enough to cause the critic St. John Ervine to give him a special mention. He was kept on in London for the next production, *Macbeth* in modern dress, and his Malcolm was striking enough to bring him out of that unhappy failure with his reputation enhanced. He was not called upon for anything of much importance in the next venture, a short season of Shaw's vast *Back to Methuselah*; but any disappointment he may have felt was amply compensated for when he found himself given the all-important name-part in Tennyson's *Harold*, which had never before been staged. He recalls with pride that he learnt the 3,000 lines of this part in one week, with the aid of a lot of coffee, heated on a small methylated spirit burner.

It proved, in fact, to be unstageable and so yet another of Jackson's experiments in that boldly experimental season came to grief; but once again Olivier had more than his share of any praise that was going. And when the season closed on a note of success with *The Taming of the Shrew*, also in modern dress, Olivier, spruce (for him) in a dinner-jacket as the Lord in the Christopher Sly scenes, was prominent in the public eye throughout the evening. Though still serving under the Birmingham banner, he had now laid the foundations of a London reputation, which were much strengthened when Jackson invited him to join the cast of *Bird in Hand* in his original part of the young squire.

This play had already been running some months at the Royalty, and was to run for seven months more—seven precious months in which to consolidate his future, which he did in more ways than one. The innkeeper's daughter was now being played by an attractive dark-haired girl, the daughter of the actor-dramatist H. V. Esmond and his wife and leading lady, Eva Moore. Jill Esmond Moore was her stage name, though she was later to shorten it to Jill Esmond. With her, according to his romantic habit, Olivier fell in love. This time no husband lurked in the background, and though their parents warned them against hasty decisions it was soon an understood thing between them that they would be married.

It may have been this prospect of a new responsibility that made him begin to take really seriously the problem of his personal appearance. During his time of acute poverty immediately after leaving the Central School he had needed all the pennies he could scrape together for the single purpose of staying alive. He could choose neither his food nor his clothing, and at one time he was reduced to wearing the cast-off suit of an uncle which had been altered to fit him but still failed to do so. With the arrival of a steady living wage had come the chance to tidy himself up a little. He must have done something about his clothes before he met Jill Esmond, for he had needed smart outfits for both of the modern-dress Shakespeare productions; but there were still his unruly hair and heavy eyebrows to be dealt with. According to Felix Barker's account it was not until the autumn of 1928 that he coped with these.

Having a date with Basil Dean on a certain important occasion, he was warned that in Dean's opinion his appearance was against him. This gave him the necessary impetus to turn up at that interview with his eyebrows plucked and his hair brushed back. There is reason to suppose that Dean was impressed; but there is chapter and verse for the impression the transformation made on Blakelock.

In his book *Advice to a Player* Blakelock brings forward Olivier as the supreme example of a man who, by application and determination, gave himself a new personality: 'He had somehow got his hair to part at last; he had the gaps between his teeth filled in; his eyebrows trimmed and straightened; and he was beautifully dressed.'

In fact, what had happened was not simply that a member of Barry Jackson's company from Birmingham had paid belated visits to his barber and his dentist. A new contender for high honour on the London stage had arrived and meant business.

Chapter 4

7. *Laurence Olivier 1930, playing a leading part in Noel Coward's new play 'Private Lives' at the Phoenix Theatre.*

The 1920's were a bad period in the London theatre. Towards the end of the First World War, when the capital had been an increasingly demoralized centre for troops on leave, the play-houses had largely fallen into the hands of managements whose only aim was to provide those troops with gaiety and glitter. Some of the light entertainment which came thus into being was brilliant, but much was tawdry and mechanical; and the serious theatre almost ceased to exist.

Even with the coming of peace-time the atmosphere of hectic excitement was not dispelled, and many of the new speculative managements remained in business hoping that there would still be easy money to be made. Only very slowly did the standard of popular taste begin to rise again, and even when it did so, it proved to have severe new limitations.

The British public, which had gone into the war in a mood of mediaeval chivalry, believing what romantic literature had told it about 'the greatest game of all', had emerged from four years of organized mass-murder battered and disillusioned. It did not know what it wanted but it knew very well that, for the time being, it did not want any more romances. It had learnt that Bernard Shaw, despised and scoffed at by all but a few both before and during the War, had shown in *Arms and the Man* that he had known better than the romanticists what war would really be like; and Shaw to his astonishment and not much to his pleasure (since he liked to be ahead of his time) found himself a popular author.

Galsworthy's solid realism had a strong appeal and so did the satirical writings of Maugham, Coward and Lonsdale; but Shakespeare and the classics were out, poetry and imaginative writing were out, costume drama was out. What the commercial managers found themselves called upon to supply was brittle contemporary comedy, as near as could be to a photographic reproduction of life on its sophisticated surface. There was, of course, a section of the public whose tastes had been formed before the War, who were devoted to the theatre as an art, and who did not allow themselves to be affected by the prevailing over-simplification; and of course there were some managements whose roots went deep and whose standards stood firm. Gradually it became clear to the critics and serious playgoers of the time that the London theatre was splitting into two separate bodies, which could be labelled for convenience 'classical' and 'modern'; and it also became clear that the two different kinds of management needed two different kinds of actor. The 'classical' managements because they were equally likely to present period or contemporary plays of the necessary quality, needed all-round, fully-trained players who were equally at home in doublet and hose or tweeds, blank verse or the latest slang. The 'modern' managers not only did not need verse-speaking, they mistrusted it. Quite a number of experienced West End actors lost their jobs about this time because it was feared that their experience in Shakespeare might invalidate them for contemporary comedy. What *was* wanted by these managements was young people, with engaging personalities, impeccable accents and easy manners, to whom contemporary realistic comedy gave a chance to behave on the stage very much as they behaved in their private lives. They came in a flood from their schools and universities, and they filled the need of the 'modern' theatre exactly. That it was a temporary need, and that many of them would find themselves out of work when the theatre re-integrated itself, did not enter their heads.

Olivier belonged, of course, both by nature and training, to the 'classic' theatre, and as one of Jackson's young men he was tagged with its label. It happened, though, that during his year in London he had not been called upon to wear that label at all conspicuously. In *Macbeth* and the *Taming of the Shrew* he had worn smart modern clothes, in *Bird in Hand* those of a country gentleman. No off-putting image of this young actor spouting verse in a toga existed in any West End manager's mind, and he was therefore able to compete on equal terms with the moderns for a part which he had set his heart on getting. This was the star-part in the stage version of P. C. Wren's novel *Beau Geste*.

The book, a highly-coloured tale of love, honour and gallantry with action shifting from an English stately home to a desert outpost of the French Foreign Legion, had had a great vogue. It was known in London theatrical circles that Basil Dean had bought the stage rights, was engaged with a collaborator in turning it into a play, and was on the look-out for a virile young actor to play the hero. It was taken for granted that the play would have a popular success commensurate with that of the book, and that the part of Beau Geste would bring both fame and fortune to the lucky actor whom Dean would choose for it.

Dean saw Olivier in *Bird in Hand* and was not impressed; later, however, he changed his mind to some extent, called him to an interview, questioned him closely. Later still he encouraged Olivier's hopes further by inviting him to a reading; but still nothing was settled. Dean wanted another opportunity to see him act. This opportunity promptly offered itself in the most timely way, for the Stage Society asked him to appear in a very different kind of war play, R. C. Sherriff's *Journey's End*, which they were to try out as one of their Sunday night productions followed by a special Monday matinée to which the Press would be invited.

Olivier accepted the engagement because it would give Dean the chance to see him as a soldier, not at all because he had any hopes of *Journey's End* itself. A realistic, disillusioned play about actual war, with no women, no romance, no glamour—how could the public be expected to come to see it? The part of Stanhope was well written, and he played it with the sincerity natural to him; but not even the excellent notices he got made him think of *Journey's End* as anything but a stalking-horse for the greater prize. And the prize was his. On the strength of his playing of Stanhope, Basil Dean offered him the part of Beau Geste after that Sunday night performance, and Olivier accepted without the least suspicion that he was throwing away the substance and grasping at a shadow.

He must have had qualms on 21st January 1929, when *Journey's End* began its spectacularly successful run at the Savoy, for by that time he was well ahead with rehearsals of *Beau Geste,* and was beginning to realize that it was a singularly bad play. It had its first night on 30th January and proved to be a quite extraordinarily bad entertainment—an experience which those who sat through it at His Majesty's are never likely to forget.

As if to punish Olivier for the mistake he had made, fate saw to it that for the next year and a half nothing went right with him. Dean gave him a leading part in *The Circle of Chalk,* a failure. Then he was in *Paris Bound* and *The Stranger Within,* both failures. Then he had what looked like a piece of luck—his first visit to New York with *Murder on the Second Floor.* But what had been a London success became a New York disaster.

There were compensations in all this, of course. He was still very young, and was becoming steadily better known to the modern as well as the classical managers. He had played a star part in one of London's finest theatres, his salary (when he had one) was steadily rising, and his notices had been consistently good, even if the plays themselves had been consistently bad. And these good notices clearly showed that the critics had not lost faith in him. All the same, he appreciated the sound sense of a remark made to him by Noel Coward in the summer of 1930: 'Look, young man, you'd better be in a success for a change.'

Coward had offered him the part of Victor in *Private Lives,* and Olivier, seeing what a dull, second-fiddle part it was, had refused it. The salary attached to it was £50 a week, his marriage to Jill Esmond was in the offing, and it does an actor no good if a

Laurence Olivier as 'Richard III' in the Old Vic production at the New Theatre, London, 1944/45.

TOP: *Laurence Olivier as 'Othello' with Maggie Smith as Desdemona in the filmed version of the National Theatre production.*

BOTTOM: *Vivien Leigh as Scarlett O'Hara with Clark Gable as Rhett Butler in David O. Selznick's 'Gone With The Wind'.*

(Metro-Goldwyn-Mayer).

run of failures goes on too long. He changed his mind, accepted Coward's offer, and promptly changed his luck too.

Because he did not want to take too much time off from his writing, Coward restricted the run of *Private Lives* to three months in London, followed by four months in New York. Still, this meant half a year's steady work, and was all the more satisfactory since Jill Esmond was given, in the New York production, the part played in London by Adrianne Allen. During this New York season, too, both the Oliviers were signed on for Hollywood to help fill the need for good speakers which the advent of the 'talkies' had brought with it.

This first visit to Hollywood was uninspiring but lucrative. He made several films, with none of which he was satisfied, though one, *Westward Passage*, led to an odd development later. After a time, however, the effects of the Great Depression began to make themselves felt among the film magnates, and a period of frustration set in. Olivier began to pine for home and the theatre. April 1933 saw him back in London playing a strong supporting part at the Playhouse in *The Rats of Norway* with Gladys Cooper. His notices were good, the play ran well, and he felt that he had regained whatever prestige his previous run of failures might have lost him; but in the middle of the run he was summoned back to Hollywood where Greta Garbo, on the strength of his playing in *Westward Passage*, had selected him as leading man in her next film.

This was an engagement too important to be turned down. Terms were arranged in a series of cables, which even included his measurements for his costumes. He obtained his release from his London commitment. He flew to Hollywood. He met Miss Garbo. He had two weeks rehearsals with her. And then the whole thing fizzled out; why, is still not certainly known. For the time being, that episode killed his interest in films stone dead. Offered a year's contract with M.G.M. which would have brought him in £12,000, he turned it down and went back to the stage, having a five-months' run in New York with *The Green Bay Tree*; and at the end of this, when he was feeling homesick and yet half-afraid to face London again after so long an absence, Noel Coward came once again to his rescue.

Coward was in New York to arrange for the London presentation of the American actress Ina Claire as the star of S. N.

9. *Laurence Olivier with Noel Coward, Gertrude Lawrence and Adrianne Allen in the London production of 'Private Lives'.*
10. *Laurence Olivier's wedding to Jill Esmond Moore, 25th July 1930.*

Behrman's *Biography*, in which she had been pleasing the Broadway public, and he invited Olivier to be her leading man. The piece did not take in London, but it served Olivier's purpose, and he found plenty of work waiting for him.

First came a call for help in emergency. Gordon Daviot's *Queen of Scots* was in rehearsal, and Ralph Richardson was finding himself so out of touch with his part as Bothwell that he implored the manager, Bronson Albery, to release him even though the production date was only eight days away. Albery asked Olivier to take over the part, and he did so; but at such short notice he could not study it very deeply, and gave a performance which somebody rudely described as 'more Hollywood than Holyrood'. The play was not even a success; nevertheless this engagement may well have proved a turning-point in Olivier's career, as will be seen.

His next offer also had its unsatisfactory side, but he dealt with it very differently. Noel Coward was producing *Theatre Royal*, by Edna Ferber and George Kaufman, for its London run. The play was a satire on the Barrymore family, and Coward asked Olivier to play the part corresponding to the eccentric and unpredictable John Barrymore, half exhibitionist, half genius. It was a part in which Olivier saw himself at once; but the trouble was that Coward only wanted him for the first two weeks on tour. He must then hand over to Brian Aherne, who would finish the tour and play the part in London. The salary offered was very good (£100 a week) but the idea of acting as a provincial stopgap for Aherne did not appeal to Olivier, and he was on the point of rejecting the offer when a bolder course occurred to him. He would accept the offer, and play the part so brilliantly that Aherne would be scared to take over from him. Something of the kind must have happened, because in fact Aherne accepted an offer to play Mercutio in New York, while Olivier in London gave a superb take-off of John Barrymore which critics said was the best thing he had yet done.

It was a personal triumph for him, and a remarkable sign of his increasing confidence in himself; but he did not get the full benefit of it. One of the eccentric pranks with which he endowed the character was a leap from a balcony, and about two months after the run began he misjudged this leap and broke his ankle. He had perforce to drop out of the cast and it was a curious coincidence that in the first play in which he was seen after his recovery—*Ringmaster*—he played a character confined to a wheel chair.

This play failed, and so did his next venture, *Golden Arrow*. This latter was a serious blow, for he had been given by Maurice Browne his first chance of trying his skill as director; and when during rehearsals there was a difference between author and manager, he had taken over the financial backing as well. It was his first experience of actor-management, and a disastrous one. Luckily, he had a film contract which enabled him to recoup his losses quickly.

With *Golden Arrow* there came to an end a section of Olivier's career in which, despite its success, he had been continually out of character. By temperament and early training he was—as already stated—essentially a 'classical' actor; yet for over six years, ever since he had left Barry Jackson's company and made a dead set at *Beau Geste,* he had been behaving like a 'modern'.

Intent on conquering the West End—that disillusioned post-war West End to which all forms of imaginative theatre were anathema—he had allowed circumstances to carry him forward as they would. Not since he left the Birmingham Repertory Theatre had he worn any but modern clothes on stage, or spoken any dialogue that was not contemporary speech, except for the short run of *Queen of Scots.* Now, however, the twenties were gone, and the gap between the two kinds of theatre was closing. John Gielgud's *Hamlet* in 1931 had shown that Shakespeare was back in popular favour. It was time for Olivier to return to his true allegiance, and the opportunity came in the autumn of 1935 when Bronson Albery, to whose rescue he had come with that under-rehearsed Bothwell, invited him to the New Theatre to act with John Gielgud, Peggy Ashcroft and Edith Evans in Gielgud's production of *Romeo and Juliet*.

Chapter 5

11. Laurence Olivier with Ralph Richardson in J. B. Priestley's 'Bees on the Boat Deck'.

With the return of popular interest in Shakespeare, much was expected of this *Romeo and Juliet* production. Albery himself said that he thought it might have a six months' run. In another man this might have seemed wild optimism, for the play had never run that long in all its history; but Albery had a deserved reputation for judgement in such matters, and in the result his forecast proved uncannily accurate. The run lasted 182 performances and broke all previous records.

The strength of the cast certainly did justify very high hopes, and these were raised still higher by the decision that Olivier and Gielgud, playing Romeo and Mercutio respectively, should exchange roles in the middle of the run, so that a number of play-goers might be tempted to visit the New Theatre twice to compare the various interpretations.

There seemed to be little cause for any anxiety. Once rehearsals began, however, Gielgud found himself very worried. He and Olivier had hardly met professionally, and never over Shakespeare, and he found Olivier's conception of the character of Romeo disconcertingly at variance with his own. He had played the part at the Old Vic not long before and its dominant quality had been exquisite speaking of the verse. Olivier, too, could speak verse well on occasion, but his interpretation of Romeo as a mere boy almost incoherent in the grip of his first adult passion did not allow for this.

Gielgud protested, but Olivier's approach to Shakespeare, his belief that the characters should be given 'reality' (by which he meant truth to human nature) before all else, and should be presented with all the vigour and virility at his command, was too strong to be uprooted by argument, for which there was in any case no time. Gielgud found that the only thing to do was to give Olivier his head, and to hope for the best.

The result was perhaps predictable. Olivier's reading of Romeo had many endearing qualities—sincerity, freshness, charm and an eager urgency—which appealed powerfully to a minority of playgoers. Most people, however, found it so far out of line with Gielgud's now familiar methods that they were upset. The general tone of the press comments was adverse, also. Even those critics who were moved by Olivier's acting felt that its very vehemence spoilt its effect.

The comparative failure of his Romeo was a shock to Olivier and badly shook his confidence for the change-over from Romeo to Mercutio later in the run. As the event proved, he need not have worried. His Mercutio—a real fantastic, a sardonic wit, as different from his boyish Romeo as possible, not only gave an early proof of the versatility which was soon to be one of his most admired characteristics but caught the taste of the town in its own right. It was acclaimed; and with Gielgud's Romeo achieving the verbal beauty that had been expected of it, the production swept on its way in complete triumph. Juliet, on her balcony, may well have mourned the more exciting of her two lovers, but for the majority of playgoers the final arrangement was the better one.

When the run of *Romeo and Juliet* was over, Olivier and Richardson, who had kept constantly in touch—Richardson had been playing Mercutio in New York, and Olivier had written to him for advice—joined forces and went into management. Their play was *Bees on the Boat-Deck,* by J. B. Priestley, then in the early tide of his success as a dramatist. It was an attractive piece in many ways, but it did not attract the public; and in the autumn of 1936 Olivier found himself recouping his losses by making a film for Alexander Korda.

Acting for the cinema still gave Olivier no pleasure, and the particular film upon which he was engaged was not destined to win him any special critical kudos. Nevertheless, it had the greatest possible effect both on his public career and his private life. The film was *Fire over England.* Vivien Leigh was playing a young maid of honour to Queen Elizabeth I, and Olivier was cast as her lover.

They had known one another as casual acquaintances for rather more than a year, but they were now thrown together in a much more intimate relationship. Korda's methods were deliberate and the film took over three months to make. The long periods when they were not on the set were spent increasingly in one another's company. By the time the picture was finished they were as much in love, whether they had confessed it to themselves or not, as the characters they had been playing.

It was during the making of this same film that Olivier's immediate stage future—and with it, as things were to turn out, the most important part of his stage career—was straightened out. It happened quite by accident as such things mostly do. Tyrone Guthrie suggested, tentatively at first but later with increasing urgency, that Olivier should join the company at the Old Vic, and take leading parts.

During the years immediately succeeding the First World War, the Old Vic, being the only London theatre with a consistent Shakespeare policy, had attracted to itself all the most knowledge-able playgoers up and down the country, to say nothing of visitors from abroad. Its audiences were famous for being the most appreciative of really good acting to be found anywhere. To appear before and to be approved by this shrewd yet responsive gathering had been the ambition of a succession of fine actors and actresses, who were only too glad to sacrifice high salaries in the West End to enjoy the experience for its own sake and to learn the lessons that it had to teach.

It had been a sort of self-propagating star system, and had been accepted without surprise by Lilian Baylis as the Almighty's answer to her prayer that He would send her good actors and let her have them cheap; but the supply had ended with Charles Laughton, for whom it was now Guthrie's task to find an adequate replacement. He had admired Olivier's work in *Romeo and Juliet*, and was ready to offer him a wide range of parts, foremost among which was Hamlet in the full four-and-a-half hour length of Shakespeare's text.

It was a rather daunting challenge, but one which an actor of courage and high ambition could not be content to evade. Evasion would have been easy enough. His future as a leading actor in the West End and in films was secure. Yet there was never any real doubt that Guthrie's offer would be accepted, even though Olivier's acceptance was cautious and slow. He reached his decision in the end after a telephone conversation with Richardson, once more in New York. He agreed to join the Old Vic Company just before Christmas 1936, and to appear in a full length production of *Hamlet* in January.

That the decision took courage is not in doubt. His Hamlet, like his Romeo, was likely to come under strong criticism for its dissimilarity to John Gielgud's recent interpretation; all the more so since it was the self-effacing modesty of Gielgud's Prince that had won the Old Vic public's heart. Olivier's task would be to win that public over to accept a prince who was a vigorous young athlete, delighting in the skill of his swordsmanship, and not at all the kind of man—on the surface, at any rate—to let himself be deterred from swift action.

There was, if he had known it, another difficulty in his way. The Old Vic public, which had not acquired its great collective reputation without generating some collective prejudices, had not liked the choice of Olivier as the key man for the new season. Steeped as they were in the dedicated atmosphere of Lilian Baylis's management, they saw Olivier as a being alien to that atmosphere—a film-star from Hollywood, a stage comedian happily at home in a bright modern satire like *The Royal Family*. Except for his recent appearances as Romeo and Mercutio, his only Shakespeare work had been in modern-dress experiments.

On the first night Guthrie, who had known of the public's

attitude but had contrived to keep his knowledge from Olivier, spent the early part of the evening on tenterhooks at the back of the auditorium. He could sense the slight hostility with which the audience watched the curtain rise, and his anxiety on the actor's behalf was acute.

It is the mark of a really good theatre audience, however, to know good acting even when it takes an unfamiliar or unexpected shape. Olivier's sincerity—that same quality that had first impressed Ellen Terry and Sybil Thorndike when they had seen him act as a young schoolboy—soon swept hostility and prejudice out of existence. He was accepted with acclamation, and need have no further troubles on that score. That night made his future.

Towards the end of the *Hamlet* rehearsals, Guthrie had asked him to choose what part he would next like to play. Olivier, with his mind frankly on his reputation for versatility and his delight in elaborate disguise, chose Sir Toby Belch; so *Twelfth Night* it was, with Jill Esmond playing Olivia. This went well, and was succeeded by *Henry V*, which was considered to be an appropriate and patriotic choice for Coronation year.

This was a tough acting test for Olivier, because he did not at all share Shakespeare's admiration for Henry. The idea of having to work himself into the skin of a character so alien to his own was not alluring. Yet, in the end, Shakespeare's sincerity appealed to the same quality in himself, and he ended by giving a performance which moved Charles Laughton to say 'You're England!'

It was during the rehearsals of *Henry V* that a new and exciting prospect opened up. Robert Jorgensen of the Danish Tourist Board made the suggestion to Lilian Baylis that the Old Vic Company should go to Denmark and perform *Hamlet* in the court-yard of Kronborg Castle at Elsinore, the mediaeval building which now stands near the spot where the historic Hamlet paced his battlements. The idea found instant favour and the visit was arranged for June.

As it turned out, this Danish trip had the effect of bringing Olivier's domestic problem to a head. The actress playing Ophelia at the Old Vic could not make the journey. During discussions about a replacement Vivien Leigh's name was mentioned, and Jorgensen, who had made his home in England and among other activities was acting as press representative at several London

12. Laurence Olivier as 'Hamlet' in the 1937 Tyrone Guthrie production at the Old Vic, London.

Angus McBean

13. *A scene from the 1937 Tyrone Guthrie production of 'Hamlet'.*
14. *Laurence Olivier as Sir Toby Belch in the 1937 Tyrone Guthrie production of 'Twelfth Night'*
at the Old Vic, London.

theatres including the Ambassadors, welcomed the suggestion that the party should include the beautiful girl at whose sensational début he had assisted two years before. She was offered the part.

It was in Denmark that she and Olivier decided that their love for each other was strong enough to justify the break-up of their existing marriages. On their return to England they broke the news, and formed a partnership which was for many years acclaimed as a spectacular success, although it did come to disaster in the end.

Vivien Leigh's position in the living theatre at this time was strange, almost unprecedented. Not even her most devoted admirers could pretend that she had much natural acting talent; but her beauty was so vivid that it alone had carried her to fame in a night. Her début had been made at the Ambassadors on 15th May 1935, in a play called *The Mask of Virtue*. The curtain had risen on a totally unknown girl gazing out into the auditorium, and the spectators, after a gasp of astonishment, had broken into a spontaneous round of applause. The fact that the subsequent performance was not very good did not prevent her from running away with the notices, or from becoming the talk of the town.

Film contracts followed, and here she was on safer ground. She had what was necessary to make her a good film actress; but on the stage her performances continued to lag behind expectation, or rather, hope. By the time she was cast for Ophelia she must have had a pretty clear idea of her limitations. She was never one to deceive herself.

Chapter 6

Angus McBean.

17. Laurence Olivier as 'Macbeth' in the 1938 Old Vic production (see page 80 for the later, Stratford, interpretation).

Although bedevilled at first by the worst of weather, the Old Vic's Elsinore season ended in glory, and was the fore-runner of many similar visits in after years. The opening performance could not be held in the stormy open air but was moved instead to an improvised stage in the ballroom of the nearby Marienlyst Hotel. The actors rose to the occasion before a sympathetic audience. By the next evening the weather had cleared and future per-formances were held, as planned, in the Castle. The Danes found Olivier's Hamlet impressive and Vivien Leigh's Ophelia easy to look at, while the visiting English critics said she was promising.

For the two players themselves the occasion was memorable as being the first time they had acted together on a stage—an experience they were not to enjoy again for some time to come. They were not far separated that autumn and winter, however, for he returned to the Old Vic to play a whole round of parts,

A scene from the National Theatre production of Congreve's 'Love For Love'. (National Theatre).

while she made a glittering Titania in Guthrie's famous Victorian *Midsummer Night's Dream* at the same theatre—though here again it was the eye that she satisfied rather than the ear.

Olivier's work during this period was of a steadily high standard, but met with varying fortune. In *Macbeth* and *Coriolanus* he made, as it were, preliminary studies in two parts in which he was to shine with a special lustre later in his career. As Iago to Richardson's Othello he suffered a disappointment; both men had long looked forward to the day when they would play these two parts together, but somehow, when the time came they did not carry it off. The comparative failure of a project so long awaited must have been a deep disappointment to Olivier, but he cannot be absolved from a large share in the blame for it. A still larger share, however, must be charged to the account of Tyrone Guthrie, who sponsored the production.

When working on the full-length *Hamlet*, in which (as already described) Olivier had made his triumphant Old Vic début, Guthrie had been much attracted by a theory put forward by an internationally famous psycho-analyst, Dr. Ernest Jones, that the reason for Hamlet's delay in revenging himself upon his uncle might well be his own subsconscious sense of guilt that he was in love with his mother. Guthrie had explained this idea to Olivier, who had worked it into his interpretation of the character. There had been a strong Freudian tinge about the Hamlet of 1937, though in the excitement of the occasion it had hardly been noticed. Now, the notion that a valuable new approach to Shakespeare might be made through modern psychological discoveries occurred once again to the minds of Guthrie and Olivier. Without telling Richardson, who they suspected might not be in sympathy, they asked Dr. Jones for his explanation of Iago's apparently motiveless hatred of Othello. This was immediately forthcoming. Iago was an unconscious homosexual who, not understanding his own perverted passion for the Moor, had twisted love into loathing.

It was, in its own way, a very plausible solution, and it impressed both Guthrie and Olivier—who would, all the same, have been much better off if they had never heard it. Their efforts to keep in line with Dr. Jones's diagnosis without offending public taste with any open suggestion of perversion turned Olivier's Iago into a character whose behaviour had the critics at a loss.

Accounts differ as to whether Richardson was let into the secret, but no version of the episode suggests that he was happy with this very unusual Iago. The fact that these two devoted friends, in this play of all plays, should be at anything less than full accord, was of itself enough to ruin the production's prospects.

Olivier finished his engagement at the Old Vic in April 1938, after which his preoccupation for the immediate future was with Hollywood. For some time Goldwyn had been trying to get him there to play Heathcliff in the film version of *Wuthering Heights*, further baiting the hook with an offer of a part in the same film for Vivien Leigh. The bait, however, was not quite tempting enough for her. She was sensibly ready to sing small in the theatre for the time being, till she could gain enough experience to try to realize her high ambitions; but in the cinema, with several starring performances behind her, she had already a reputation and prestige to lose. To accept Goldwyn's offer of the secondary part of Isabella would be to take a step down, which neither she nor Olivier thought wise. He therefore undertook to play Heathcliff if Vivien Leigh could have the leading part, Cathy; otherwise he was not interested. But Cathy had been virtually promised to Merle Oberon.

Olivier's real reason for refusing to go without Vivien Leigh was his reluctance to be parted from her so soon after they had come together. She knew this and also that the part of Heathcliff had a real attraction for him. She argued that such partings were and must be a necessary evil, and must not be allowed to interfere with their professional lives. She herself had two London engagements—*Serena Blandish* at the Gate and a revival of *A Midsummer Night's Dream* at the Old Vic. She thought he should accept the Hollywood offer, and go alone. After all, it would only be for three months. He agreed, and sailed early in November.

In Hollywood, things did not go smoothly. He found himself at odds with Goldwyn, with Merle Oberon, and with his director, William Wyler. His letters home were so full of misery that Vivien Leigh took a wild decision to dash out to see him. She could raise enough money to pay for the trip and she had just time enough to reach Hollywood, spend five days there, and then dash back to England in time to rehearse Titania. She sent a cable to

46

18. *Laurence Olivier as Iago in the 1938 production of 'Othello' at the Old Vic.* Angus McBean.

say she was coming, and sailed in the *Queen Mary*.

The sequel to this incident is almost too coincidentally dramatic to be believed. At the moment when she arrived in Hollywood the film version of the celebrated best-selling novel *Gone With the Wind* was just going into production in spite of the fact that the key part of Scarlett O'Hara had not been cast. When Olivier got Vivien Leigh's cable, he remembered that she had been fascinated by the charactor of Scarlett when the novel first appeared in England and had wished she had a chance to play the part. Here *was* a chance—a distant one, but still a chance. He pulled the necessary strings, which resulted in her meeting the right people and being given the right tests. Her five-days' stay had to be extended while the tests were being evaluated, and she cabled to Guthrie in London. He released her from her Old Vic engagement, and on Christmas Day 1938 she learnt that she had been given the part.

That this much publicized prize should be carried off by an 'unknown' English girl made news everywhere, so Vivien Leigh had the experience of sudden fame for the second time in her short life. She signed her contract with David Selznick (it was for seven years) and started work in January. The film took five months to make and it was only for the first ten weeks or so of this time that she could go to Olivier for help or advice. Once *Wuthering Heights* was completed he felt that he must take the opportunity to re-establish himself on the stage of Broadway, so towards the end of March he left to join Katharine Cornell in S. N. Behrman's *No Time for Comedy,* which opened in New York in April. It was now Vivien Leigh's turn to endure alone and as best she could the rigours of Hollywood film-making and the constant chopping and changing of text, the coming and going of directors, the lack of any continuity in the shooting of scenes, that working on *Gone With The Wind* entailed.

'How I *hate* film-acting,' she said in a desperate letter home. On the whole, though, she enjoyed acting Scarlett O'Hara, and when all was over said good-bye to the character with regret.

Olivier, it is interesting to note, no longer hated film-acting or looked upon it as merely a source of large quantities of ready cash. Once his initial lack of sympathy with William Wyler had worn off, he had realized that the director had much to teach him, and

19. *Laurence Olivier with Merle Oberon in the William Wyler film of 'Wuthering Heights'.*
20. *Laurence Olivier with Greer Garson in 'Pride and Prejudice'.* Samuel Goldwyn Productions.

Metro-Goldwyn-Mayer

by the time *Wuthering Heights* was finished had developed a new respect for the medium and a belief that he might himself come to do good work in it, as actor or director or both.

For the time being, however, all he was to get from it was acute embarrassment. While he was playing in *No Time For Comedy*, the release of *Wuthering Heights* took place. It was a great popular success and he found himself bereft of all privacy. Reporters badgered him at every turn, and at the stage door of the Ethel Barrymore Theatre he was besieged by crowds of fans whose object seemed to be to tear him to pieces. His reaction to this was indignant and far from tactful. His attitude, unusual in New York, was denounced as outrageous, and he was made the victim of a virulent press campaign, which he had to bear as best he might. He was glad enough to escape for a holiday in England with Vivien Leigh after she had joined him in New York when her film was finished.

This holiday over, they returned together to Hollywood, sailing from Southampton in August. War was threatening, but the threat seemed rather less insistent than it had a year before at the time of the Munich episode, and both had commitments difficult to cancel. They set sail hopefully, but this time Hitler was determined to have his war.

When it started the younger members of the British colony in Hollywood were in some doubt as to where their immediate duty lay, most wishing to return at once to England. However, an official directive was sent to them through the British consul's office in Los Angeles informing them that, for the time being, they were to stay put and get on with their jobs. This left Olivier free to make two films—*Rebecca* and *Pride and Prejudice*—while Vivien Leigh was busy with retakes for *Gone With The Wind*.

Then this marathon production was at last finished and in December 1939 had its first public showing, with an impact that was felt all over the world. The actress who had played Scarlett was acclaimed as a great star. Her success in the world of cinema was far greater than Olivier's in *Wuthering Heights*, and in the Hollywood enclave she now ranked above him. To Hollywood's astonishment, however, this caused no change in her professional attitude towards him. She still deferred to his superior talent, experience and judgement.

50

21. Laurence Olivier with Joan Fontaine in Alfred Hitchcock's film of 'Rebecca'.

22. Laurence Olivier with Vivien Leigh in their first great film success, Alexander Korda's production of 'Lady Hamilton'.

David O. Selznick.

London Films.

The truth about Vivien Leigh at this time seems to have been that she still thought of the cinema as Olivier had till lately thought of it, as an easy way to big money and useful publicity, but as no more than that. Her real ambition lay, and was always to lie, in the living theatre. She wanted to be a good, even (if possible) a great, stage actress, and in Olivier she saw not only the man with whom she had fallen in love, but an actor destined for the theatrical heights, a man who could help her share those heights with him; and because of his devotion to her would want to do so.

That he did want to do so was made clear almost at once. Early in 1940, during the filming of *Pride and Prejudice*, he had the idea that with a new, brilliant production of *Romeo and Juliet* they could establish themselves on Broadway as an acting team of the first rank. He began to lay plans for this, and as the war had not yet made Atlantic sailings dangerous, it was easy, though certainly expensive, to bring over the London firm of Motley and give them virtual *carte blanche* to design an elaborate permanent setting and gorgeous costumes. Once started, he proceeded on a lavish scale, risking on this one throw all the money the two of them had made in Hollywood.

They opened in San Francisco, to crowded houses and, on the whole, favourable criticism, and after a short tour arrived in May in New York, in high hopes that their work would please the critics and draw the more discriminating public, who had in any case made encouragingly heavy advance bookings. They opened at the 51st Street Theatre, and met dire and instantaneous disaster.

Much of the New York criticism was not merely adverse, it was hostile. Unknown to Olivier, Broadway had an ancient grudge against Hollywood, and here was a production bearing the brand of Hollywood plain upon it. What the notices showed was an almost total resentment that two film-stars, one with little stage experience and a stranger to Broadway, should try to use the New York stage and a grandiose and inadequate Shakespearean spectacle as a means of cashing in on Hollywood reputations.

More fatal even than this was Brooks Atkinson's notice in *The New York Times*. His integrity was such that no suspicion of prejudice or resentment could lie against him, and he, though

23. *Laurence Olivier and Vivien Leigh, with Alexander Knox, in their ill-fated production of 'Romeo and Juliet', New York, 1940.*

not hostile like some others, was equally adverse. He complained that the play had been sacrificed to over-elaborate production, that it had been set so far upstage that it was largely inaudible, and had nowhere captured the heat and passion of the tragedy.

Feeling that all this was too bad to be true, Olivier rang up the theatre to find out whether there was any public reaction, and was told that a long queue had formed extending right round the building; but before he could extract any comfort from this he was further told that the queue consisted of people who had booked in advance and were now asking for their money back. What, asked the box-office manager, was to be done? 'Return their money,' said Olivier, and in that moment of hurt pride, he made a decision he was later to regret, for it only added financial ruin to artistic failure.

But personal disaster, however complete, could not weigh in comparison with the general catastrophe of which news was brought by the same papers in which the notices of *Romeo and Juliet* had appeared. In France the Germans were breaking through to the Channel, and England was seriously threatened with invasion. All through the four miserable weeks of the *Romeo and Juliet* run, weeks during which money drained away at the rate of £250 a night, the news from home grew worse and worse, and the problem of what to do about it grew more insistent. The official view was still that English people abroad should stay where they were, but inaction in such circumstances was intolerable to a man of Olivier's temperament. He had had a little flying experience, and he wrote to Ralph Richardson, now serving with the Fleet Air Arm, asking if there would be an opening there for him. Also he cabled to Duff Cooper, a personal friend who was now Minister of Information, asking if he should return home, and got in reply a rather mysterious instruction not to hurry home as he might be more useful where he was. Richardson's reply also discouraged immediate return, as the age-limit for inexperienced men was 28 and Olivier was now 33. He asked if Olivier could get some flying practice in America before returning home, as older men were accepted according to their experience.

This frustrating period was brought suddenly to an end by a telephone message from Alexander Korda, with a proposal which made sense of Duff Cooper's cable. Speaking from Hollywood, he said he was over in America to make a patriotic film about Lord Nelson. He wanted Olivier for Nelson and Vivien Leigh for Lady Hamilton, and said that shooting on the film would start in September. This timely offer solved their immediate problems— duty and money—and gave Olivier the chance he needed to have some flying lessons and get his pilot's licence. And as if to underline the fact that their luck really had turned, August brought them the news that their divorces were through.

They were married on 30th August 1940, just before the start of the Lady Hamilton film, and they sailed for home soon after it was finished, arriving in blacked-out and battered England just after the turn of the year.

Chapter 7

25. *Laurence Olivier in his film of 'Henry V'.*   J. Arthur Rank Organization.

Considering the trouble and the risks which Olivier had taken to fit himself for the Fleet Air Arm—he had crashed three times during his California course, but had escaped whole—his actual service with that organization did not give him much satisfaction. The 200 hours of solo flying he had done in America qualified him for a commission as sub-lieutenant in the R.N.V.R. but did not serve to make him an operational pilot; and as a second-line man he found himself allotted a number of dull, routine duties some of which did not get him into the air at all.

At last, in despair, he volunteered to fly a Walrus, and was accepted. This was a small airplane whose function was to be catapulted from battleships, and when she heard of the prospect ahead, Vivien Leigh was understandably worried. But even here he was unlucky (or lucky, depending on the point of view). Before he had finished his special training for this job, Walruses were taken out of service.

Meanwhile, in departments of the war effort less accustomed than the Navy to the stern demands of discipline, the word went round that Olivier was stationed within easy reach and that his services could be borrowed. Very soon his harassed commanding officer learnt how difficult it is to keep duty-rosters functioning smoothly if one of your junior duty-officers is a leading actor and world-famous film star. Olivier was increasingly in demand, and, once it had been finally established that he would not be required for operational flights against the enemy, he himself felt no qualms at being given temporary release to make films. This state of affairs reached its culminating point in 1943, when he was asked to direct the film version of Shakespeare's *Henry V*, with himself in the name-part.

What he himself thought of all this may perhaps be deduced from his entry in *Who's Who in the Theatre,* where no mention whatever is made of his service in the R.N.V.R. After recording the New York *Romeo* in 1940 he remarks drily 'spent the next three years making films', and then goes straight on to chronicle his return to the stage in 1944.

In none of this was there a place for Vivien Leigh. When first Olivier went into uniform she settled down to play the part of a naval officer's wife; but after a time she saw that she could quite easily combine this with doing a play in London. Olivier picked out for her the part of Mrs. Dubedat in Shaw's *The Doctor's Dilemma,* and the play was staged by Tennent's at the Haymarket Theatre in March 1942. It ran for more than a year, and showed a great advance in her powers as an actress, besides being totally different from Scarlett O'Hara, with whom she was in some danger of being for ever identified.

Her long run finished while Olivier was planning his *Henry V* film, and he took it for granted that his wife would play Princess Katharine—a small part, but very charming, and, once again, a complete contrast to Scarlett. Here, however, it was necessary to get Selznick's permission, and this was flatly refused. Selznick had not been best pleased by his star's action in turning her back on Hollywood and going home to England, and this may have coloured his refusal; but there was sense in his argument that people would not expect to see the star of *Gone with the Wind* in an insignificant part.

Henry V, filmed in Ireland, was a lavish affair, and cost a great deal more than the £300,000 which had been the original estimate. There were long and apprehensive faces among the people responsible for its finances, but in the end all was well. It was a great success in England, and a still greater one in America where it won Olivier an Oscar; but that award must have seemed of small consequence to him by the time it was made, for by then he was taking part in an enterprise which still ranks in the memory of those who saw it as one of the great achievements of the theatre in Britain.

The Old Vic Company, long exiled in Lancashire and unable to get back to London because its theatre had been bombed, had been promised by Bronson Albery, who was joint administrator of the Old Vic with Tyrone Guthrie, that they could have the New Theatre in the autumn of 1944. For such an enterprise as a West End season in one of London's most important theatres, the company would need to be built up to the greatest strength possible, and Guthrie invited Ralph Richardson to help with the task. Richardson agreed, on two conditions—that he could get his release from the Fleet Air Arm, in which he was now a Lieutenant-Commander, and that he could have the assistance of John Burrell, a drama producer from the B.B.C.; and together Richardson and Burrell went to see Olivier at Denham, where he was putting the finishing touches to *Henry V,* and persuaded him to join them.

The Admiralty released Richardson and Olivier with an alacrity which the latter described as 'almost hurtful', and the two of them and Burrell were appointed joint directors of the company, and proceeded to make theatre history, the first step towards which was to engage a company in which were stalwarts like Sybil Thorndike, Harcourt Williams, Nicholas Hannen and George Relph, with promising newcomers like Michael Warre, Joyce Redman and Margaret Leighton.

They had chosen an uncomfortable time to begin. When the decision had been made to bring the company back to London, it had seemed that all danger from the air was over; but with the invention of the flying bomb and the V-rocket the Germans, though now close to defeat, had been able to resume their bom-

26. *Laurence Olivier with Eric Portman in '49th Parallel', the first film he made while in the Navy.*
27. *A scene from Olivier's film production of 'Henry V'.*

J. Arthur Rank Organization.

bardment in a manner both destructive and unnerving. Concentration on rehearsals in such conditions was not easy, nor did the prospect look bright for a successful season—badly needed because the Old Vic was financially in a very bad way. The best hope was that the allied armies advancing through Normandy might capture the bases from which these missiles were being launched, and in the event this did in fact happen. The last flying bomb of the war was sent on its way just two days before the Old Vic opened with *Peer Gynt*.

The plan of the Old Vic campaign was that each of the two leading men should choose himself a big classical part, and that there should be a third play of lighter texture in which both could appear to advantage. Richardson had come to conference with his mind already made up. He wanted to play Peer Gynt in Ibsen's sprawling masterpiece; and he did play it to admiration, giving the season a flying start. Olivier played the tiny but effective part of the Button-Moulder, a symbolic character with only one short scene.

The lighter play was Shaw's *Arms and the Man*, Richardson playing Bluntschli (which he liked) and Olivier Sergius (which at first he did not). The part as written is pure caricature, and he made the initial mistake of trying to turn it into a portrait; but if Sergius is taken in the least seriously he becomes intolerable. Some adverse notices during a try-out week in Manchester brought this home to him, and in London he played the part for laughs, and all went well.

The part of the Button-Moulder was a wise, indeed a cunning, choice. Not only did it give him a chance to ease his way back on to the stage after an excessive dose of cinema, it also earned him praise for his modesty and his readiness to accept repertory conditions. But neither the Button-Moulder nor Sergius constituted a come-back for an actor of his eminence, and it was therefore all the more important that his choice of a star part for himself should be a right one.

Unlike Richardson, he had had no character in mind that he specially wanted to play, and when Burrell suggested Richard III his first reaction had been adverse. Donald Wolfit had made a success in this part not long before, and it would be disastrous if he, Olivier, allowed himself to be compared to his disadvantage

A recent photograph of Olivier taken during rehearsals at the National Theatre. (National Theatre).

Laurence Olivier with Joan Plowright and Celia Johnson in the National Theatre production of Ibsen's 'The Master Builder'. *(National Theatre)*.

with a fellow-actor with whom, anyhow, he did not want to seem to be in competition. In every other way, however, the part was exactly what he needed. Finally he decided to do it because he could think of no better idea. In the outcome, there was no question of comparison or competition—Olivier's Richard proved to have about it a transcendent quality which set it outside such considerations.

Somebody once said that the finest opening to any play ever written was that in which Richard III limps downstage to deliver the great speech of self-avowal which begins:

'Now is the winter of our discontent
Made glorious summer by this sun of York'

It was as if Olivier had read this comment and had set himself to prove its truth. As he made his way downstage, very slowly and with odd interruptions in his progress, he seemed malignity incarnate. All the complications of Richard's character—its cruelty, its ambition, its sardonic humour—seemed implicit in his expression and his walk, so that when at last he reached the front of the stage and began the speech, all that he had to say of his evil purpose seemed to us in the audience less like a revelation than a confirmation of something we had already been told. This was the prelude to a performance which not only made a new reputation for the actor, but set the seal upon this Old Vic season as an adventure in playgoing. Something, it was felt, had returned to the stage which had long been lost. Was it, perhaps, great acting?

This was a question which was to be more widely and insistently asked during the next two years. The company's record of success was not unbroken—a production of *Uncle Vanya* was below standard, and was not included in the repertory when, in the summer of 1944, the company went overseas to entertain the troops and was accorded the unique honour of being invited to play a fortnight at the Comédie Française in newly liberated Paris. But the general quality of the acting was as high in the second season at the New Theatre as it had been in the first, and Richardson's magnificent Falstaff, in a production which presented Parts I and II of *Henry IV* in chronological order, was hailed as a further example of the grand manner, as was Olivier's Oedipus.

Olivier, it is true, came under adverse criticism with some

29. *Laurence Olivier as Sergius with Margaret Leighton as Raina in the Old Vic production of* '*Arms and the Man*'.

John Vickers.

32. *Laurence Olivier as Astrov in the Old Vic production of 'Uncle Vanya' (see title page for the later, National Theatre, interpretation).*

33. *Laurence Olivier with Ralph Richardson, Margaret Leighton and Joyce Redman in 'Uncle Vanya'.*
John Vickers.

John Vickers.

people for his choice of a companion piece to the *Oedipus Rex,* which, like all Greek tragedies, made a very short evening's entertainment. He chose *The Critic* and himself took the part of Mr. Puff. The objectors acknowledged the tremendous emotional climax to which he had swept Sophocles's self-blinded hero, but felt that it was a mistake for the actor to reappear a matter of minutes later in a funny false nose to play Sheridan's ridiculous invention.

It had been all very well, they argued, for him to indulge his pride in his own versatility and his love of disguise with a rather similar contrast in *King Henry IV,* by playing a manly and vital Hotspur in Part I and a practically senile Justice Shallow in Part II, but in that case a decent interval elapsed between the two impersonations, whereas the Oedipus/Mr. Puff transition smacked of a quick-change turn in a music-hall.

Malcontents were a tiny minority, however. Versatility is a stage quality that has a strong popular appeal, and here was versatility of a very high order and at a very high level. And few were found to deny that this Oedipus, was a *tour-de-force* which, taken in conjunction with Richard III, gave him a powerful claim to be considered the best serious actor on the contemporary British stage, a claim which neither Gielgud nor Richardson could any longer match.

A visit by the company to America immediately after the spring of 1946 served to strengthen this opinion. Absurdly over-done preliminary publicity had had two quite different effects in New York. The playgoing public, assured that it was about to see an exhibition of ensemble acting with which the Moscow Art Theatre could hardly have competed, made a mad rush for tickets. The critics, justly suspicious of advertising build-ups, were on the cool side and George Jean Nathan, best practitioner in the 'you-can't-fool-me' school of criticism, pointed out—quite correctly, but with unnecessary rudeness—that the Old Vic Company was not an ensemble at all in the Moscow sense of the word. Yet even the critics' guard was not proof against Olivier's Oedipus. Every paper in New York joined in his praise; and John Mason Brown, weighing the word with a jeweller's care, said that this was a truly 'great' piece of acting.

In none of these high matters did Vivien Leigh play more than

34. Laurence Olivier as Hotspur in Part I of the Old Vic production of 'King Henry IV'.

35. Laurence Olivier as Justice Shallow with Ralph Richardson as Sir John Falstaff in Part II of 'King Henry IV'.

John Vickers.

John Vickers.

36. *Laurence Olivier as Mr. Puff, in 'The Critic'.*
37. *'The Critic', the final moment of the play.*

John Vickers.

John Vickers.

a spectator's part, for during the years 1944–46 she had concerns of her own to attend to. At the time of the Old Vic's return to London she was engaged in the making of the film version of Shaw's *Caesar and Cleopatra* with which Gabriel Pascal had hoped to repeat his success with *Pygmalion*. She had the satisfaction of finding that her work as Cleopatra showed an increase of technical skill in her acting, but this was her only satisfaction, as the picture proved a costly and time-wasting failure. As soon as she was free of it she moved on to a much more rewarding project—her return to the stage in a star part, that of Sabina in Thornton Wilder's allegorical fantasy, *The Skin of our Teeth*, a play which Olivier had found for her and a part with which she had fallen in love.

Under her husband's direction, and H. M. Tennent's management she had opened in this on 16th May 1945 at the Phoenix Theatre and had scored a complete personal triumph. She showed a vitality, a confidence, a lightness of touch and above all a sense of comedy which the London critics had not known she possessed and were delighted to welcome. How much she owed to Olivier's example, direction and influence and how much to her own determination, intelligence and hard work is a point often debated and never resolved, but the result was not in doubt—she was now an actress good enough to take her place by his side as leading lady.

Triumph was followed by an unhappy setback. Towards the end of a longish run as Sabina she began to feel tired and ill, and it was discovered that she had a tubercular patch on one lung. This proved less serious than was at first feared, but after finishing the run of the play she had to spend six weeks in hospital and several months in bed. She was, however, pronounced a cure in time to accompany Olivier and the Old Vic Company on the American visit 'just for the ride'.

The Old Vic's autumn season of 1946 at the New Theatre saw yet one more major performance from Olivier—his King Lear. This did not call forth unanimous critical acclaim, but it was nevertheless a fine achievement, which in remembrance has been rated too low. He brought to it, as to all his Shakespearean characterizations, a fresh eye and a determination to make the part as real as possible. This was seen particularly in that difficult scene where Lear divides his kingdom. Here was no senile

dodderer, but a vigorous old tyrant with a streak of grim humour as well as a streak of madness, tired of responsibility and ready to hand it over, but too self-sufficient to realize that with responsibility he must inevitably shed power.

This was admirable, and to some critics what followed was equally admirable; to others, the later scenes of downfall and madness were not deeply moving. Lear has been very well acted in our time, and it is probably true to say that this is why Olivier's performance has been dimmed a little in retrospect. It has to be remembered as one among several notable Lears; it has not the transcendent quality of his Richard III or his Oedipus.

39. 'King Lear', a scene from the Old Vic production.   John Vickers.

Chapter 8

40. *Laurence Olivier in his film production of 'Hamlet'.* Rank Organization.

After *King Lear,* Olivier turned his mind for a space to matters outside the Old Vic. It had been part of his arrangement with the Governors that he could take time off to make a film, and ever since *Henry V* he had been under pressure to do another Shakespeare picture. Late in 1946 this pressure was intensified, and he decided to yield to it and do a screen version of *Hamlet* with himself in the name part.

To reduce so huge a play to a manageable length, and to simplify it so that the cinema public could follow it, involved drastic cutting and even some interference with the text. What with elaborate preparations and the actual making of the film, Olivier found his time very fully occupied for almost the whole of 1947. The result was a picture which, predictably, did not much please lovers of Shakespeare; but to those who had never read *Hamlet* or seen it on the stage it seemed wonderful. It more than repeated the success of *Henry V,* and won for Olivier an inter-

72

national award as well as another Oscar.

It was during the making of this film that he learnt that he was to be given a knighthood in the birthday honours, and while this could not have been a complete surprise since Ralph Richardson had already been knighted at the New Year, it was a gratifying culmination to the exciting doings of the past years. Shortly afterwards, there was another proof of the respect in which his work was held in official circles. He was invited by the British Council to lead an Old Vic company in a lengthy tour of Australia and New Zealand, with Vivien Leigh as his leading lady. The tour was to start as soon as his film was finished.

Here was a chance of acting together such as the Oliviers had long looked for. Touring in the Antipodes would mean many long journeys and much careful organization; it would be a tiring assignment; but with his abounding vitality and her restored health they could face it. They needed three plays—a starring vehicle for him *(Richard III)*: one for her *(The Skin of our Teeth)*: and a third play in which both could shine, for which purpose Olivier chose *The School for Scandal,* thinking that his wife would make an enchanting Lady Teazle; while Sir Peter was a part with a particular appeal for him.

They had some argument over this because, unexpectedly, she saw nothing in the part; but in the end she deferred to his maturer judgement. Her other choice, Sabina in the Wilder play, was forced upon them. The play itself, with its obscurities and its symbolism (it was described by its author in a sub-title as 'A History of Mankind in Comic Strip') might not be suitable for audiences inexperienced in such productions, but it was the only one in which she had yet given a stage performance of the star quality that would be expected of her.

However, on arrival in Australia they found that any anxieties they may have felt on such matters were swallowed up in a greater anxiety, how to stay the course mapped out for them. As twin film stars making a personal appearance they aroused unassuageable excitement in the general public wherever they went; and on top of that, as official guests under the aegis of the British Council they were faced with a list of social engagements which left them no time for rest or quiet. The whole tour was a triumph, but it lasted seven months and both its leaders came near to being killed by kindness. Towards the end of it, Olivier was acting on crutches because of an injured knee. But the tour's most upsetting moment was no doing of their enthusiastic hosts. It had come when, in Sydney, Olivier received a letter from Lord Esher, chairman of the Governors of the Old Vic. It was a very polite letter, but among the compliments one plain fact refused to be concealed. At the end of their five years' contract—which was to say after the spring season of 1949—the three directors would not be re-appointed. It was a highly decorated and totally unexpected dismissal.

What the internal politics were that led the Governors to make this move has never been made public, and a short biography of this nature is no place in which to explore the various conjectures. Here it must suffice to say that to most interested people their action seemed at the time ungracious as well as ungrateful and in retrospect a classic example of the folly of throwing away substance in order to grasp at shadow. The three 'retiring' directors (there was a pretence in public, which took nobody in, that they were laying down their work voluntarily) had raised the Old Vic to a point where it had a chance to become the long-wished-for National Theatre, and had made long-term plans which would have carried on its development in that direction. The Governors announced that the changes in administration were a step towards the preparation of a National Theatre, but the step turned out to be a very bad stumble by which progress was brought to an ignominious halt.

If the Governors were not particularly pleased to see Olivier home again, the public was; and on the day in January 1949 when he opened at the New Theatre in *The School for Scandal* it welcomed him in every possible way—thronging the box-office, sleeping on the St. Martin's Lane pavements to get unreserved seats, holding up the traffic on the off-chance of getting a glimpse of him or his leading lady. Any resentment he was feeling must have melted at least temporarily in the warmth of it all.

In any case, the Oliviers shared a personal reason why this particular first night was to be reckoned a special occasion—it was the first time they had ever acted together on the West End stage. It was a little unfortunate, of course, that Vivien Leigh was still not happy in her part, though Olivier was convinced that she

41. *A scene from the Old Vic production of 'Antigone'.*

42. *Laurence Olivier and Vivien Leigh in their St. James's Theatre production of 'Caesar and Cleopatra'.*

had it in her to be the great Lady Teazle of her time. She was good enough to get by, however. The critics made it clear that they enjoyed looking at this Lady Teazle better than listening to her, but they were polite. Over her next performance they were much more polite, and by an odd contrast it was in a part that Olivier had not wanted her to attempt. It was the sombre Antigone in Jean Anouilh's play of that name, and called for a power of which even her husband did not think her capable. What with this, and what with his reappearance as Richard III, their Old Vic engagement was brought to a full close.

Once again his own master, he decided to gratify old ambition and become his own master in good earnest, by launching out as an actor-manager. Immersed in preparations for this, he did no more acting that year, though his name did appear once on a play-bill when, in the autumn, he directed Vivien Leigh in *A Streetcar Named Desire*. As with Sabina, she had fallen in love with the part of the doomed Blanche Du Bois when first she read Tennessee Williams's play; and on the strength of her Antigone he had no doubt that it lay within her range. He carried her to complete success in it, and with the help of a public controversy over some aspects of the piece which were, to many people, profoundly shocking, it acquired curiosity value and ran for 326 performances. On the strength of this, she was invited to play the same part in the Hollywood film version made by Warner Brothers in 1950. Starring opposite Marlon Brando, she won another Oscar to put beside the one she had been given for *Gone with the Wind*.

One result of this was that when Olivier, having acquired a lease of the St. James's Theatre, opened there on 18th January 1950, as the Duke in Christopher Fry's *Venus Observed*, the part originally written for Vivien Leigh could not be played by her—which was probably just as well since it was a young girl part of a kind in which she no longer saw herself.

Be that as it may, the first part in which she did appear at the St. James's, in May 1951, was that of a very young girl indeed; Cleopatra in Shaw's *Caesar and Cleopatra*. The occasion was the opening of the Festival of Britain, in aid of which every theatre-manager in London was expected to do his utmost; and Olivier had decided, after anxious discussion, that his contribution to the

Laurence Olivier in the National Theatre production of Strindberg's 'Dance of Death'. (National Theatre).

cause would be the joint presentation of two Cleopatra plays, with Vivien Leigh first as Shaw's kitten and then as Shakespeare's mature queen, with himself playing Caesar to the first and Antony to the second. The idea found much favour and the production much praise, both in London and in New York whither it was transferred later in the year.

When the two plays went into rehearsal Olivier discovered that in the intensity of his search, as manager, for material suitable for a special occasion, he had neglected to some extent his own best interests as actor. Neither Shaw's Caesar nor Shakespeare's Antony ranks as a bad acting part, but he was not happy with either of them. He found Caesar boring and Antony weak; and as it was always a misery to him to be miscast he was much below his best in both parts.

This was widely remarked, and a wrong interpretation was put upon it which caught the public fancy at the time and remains an article of belief to this day. It was said that Olivier was deliberately 'playing down' both parts so that Vivien Leigh's acting as Cleopatra might seem more brilliant by comparison.

He himself would have none of this. He felt, and still feels, that the very suggestion was an insult to his own integrity as an artist and a patronizing denigration of his wife's acting powers. He points out too, with great cogency, that it would not be possible to play Caesar underneath the little Cleopatra, because Shaw makes it very clear as the play goes on, that Caesar is the only character in whom he has any interest. From half-way through the middle act Cleopatra is given nothing to say that is remotely amusing.

All the same, the idea took root, all the more strongly because those two plays did indeed mark the beginning of a period of four years when Olivier, in his middle forties when he should have been displaying his powers at their very peak, seemed to have lost interest in his own acting. It was not in his nature to be idle; he was a very busy man indeed during those four years, but the work in which he was absorbed was that of a theatre-manager, presenting plays in which he himself appeared neither as actor nor as director. The most interesting of these productions was the Orson Welles *Othello* (June 1951).

Once only during that time did he leave his office for the arena.

43. *Laurence Olivier as Mark Antony in 'Antony and Cleopatra' at the St. James's Theatre.*

44. *Laurence Olivier, Vivien Leigh, Martita Hunt and company in Terence Rattigan's 'The Sleeping Prince'.*

Angus McBean.

Angus McBean.

That was in 1953, when he was invited to direct his wife and himself in Terence Rattigan's *The Sleeping Prince* at the Phoenix Theatre. His admirers were delighted at the prospect of seeing him in action again, but their hopes were once again dashed, for it seemed that he was still holding to his alleged purpose of highlighting his wife's performance and keeping his own in shadow. She had the showy part of a gay young American girl whom a Teutonic princeling wants to make his mistress. Olivier played this character with his usual skill but made him, so it was thought, unnecessarily charmless. The play was not a failure, for it ran for eight months; but this could hardly be reckoned a success by Olivier's standards, let alone Rattigan's.

The reason for this disconcerting gap in the career of so eminent an actor is a matter for conjecture but is probably quite simple. Olivier was a man of enormous energy and wide-ranging ambition. He wanted to be a great actor; he wanted to nurse Vivien Leigh's lesser but still considerable talent so that she could act with him on level terms; he wanted to be a notable director; and now, in addition, he wanted to become a presenting manager with a reputation for discrimination. He was also deeply committed both as director and as actor to his work for the films. Not even his vitality would have been equal to the strain of following five different careers at once, and it is arguable that during the four-year 'gap' he deliberately elected to drop the activity in which he felt safest in order to learn thoroughly the one in which his experience was small. If that is a true guess, his time was not wasted. His years as impresario must have counted heavily in his favour when, a few years later, the Governors of the National Theatre made him their choice as director.

Corroborative evidence that this guess may be right is to be found in the assured mastery with which he resumed his acting career in April 1955, when he and Vivien Leigh were invited to play leading parts in three plays at what was then known as the Shakespeare Memorial Theatre at Stratford-upon-Avon.

He led off with a Malvolio whom, characteristically, he denuded of traditional trappings and presented as a realistic study of a self-righteous and ambitious underling—'a Roundhead among Cavaliers', somebody said of him—who allowed vanity to cloud his judgement. He followed this in June with *Macbeth*. Here he

45. *Laurence Olivier in 'Twelfth Night' at Stratford-upon-Avon.*

46. *Laurence Olivier and Vivien Leigh in 'Macbeth' at Stratford-upon-Avon.* Angus McBean.

Angus McBean.

47. *Laurence Olivier and Vivien Leigh in 'Titus Andronicus' at Stratford-upon-Avon. Their subsequent tour in this production was to prove their last appearance together.* Angus McBean.

reached the very core of the character—that of a bad man with enough imagination to know how much better off he would have been as a good one—and gave a performance which remains in the memory of those who saw it as the best Macbeth of our time. Then, in August, he threw himself with enthusiasm into the piled-up horrors of the seldom-seen *Titus Andronicus*, playing the name-part under Peter Brook's direction.

For Vivien Leigh, this Stratford season was less than triumphant. Her Viola was attractive but not moving, and for Lady Macbeth she was not considered to carry the necessary guns, though Olivier himself disagrees strongly with this verdict. He found her 'most satisfying' in the part. The ill-used Lavinia in *Titus* was well within her range, but the acting chances given by the part virtually end in Act II, when Lavinia is raped and mutilated; after that, the action shifts away from her, and all the actress can do is to look pretty and pathetic.

1956 saw no new stage venture on Olivier's part, except the presentation of an Australian company in the Australian play, *The Summer of the Seventeenth Doll*, but it brought him the British Film Academy Award for his film version of *Richard III*. Early in 1957, however, he appeared at the Royal Court, where his old friend George Devine was beginning to make a page of contemporary stage history with his sponsorship of what came to be known as the new wave of British drama. Olivier's part was that of Archie Rice in John Osborne's *The Entertainer*, a broken-down third-rate music-hall 'comic'; and it must have presented an irresistible challenge to his love of disguise and of contrast. At any rate he brought off a personal triumph of such brilliance that it tended to obscure the author's intention of making the deplorable Archie symbolic of England in the mid-1950s.

In June of the same year he revived *Titus Andronicus*, once again under the direction of Peter Brook, and took it for a quick Continental tour which included Paris, Venice, Belgrade, Zagreb, Vienna and Warsaw; and finally brought it back to London, where it was the last production to be staged at the Stoll before that theatre was demolished. Vivien Leigh played her old part of Lavinia, and that was the last time husband and wife were ever to act together. They separated soon afterwards, and in due course their marriage was dissolved.

Chapter 9

48. *Laurence Olivier in the film version of John Osborne's 'The Entertainer'.*   British Lion

In the hectically busy kind of life that Olivier and Vivien Leigh were living at this time, domestic crises have to be taken as they come. In September 1957 Olivier was acting in *The Entertainer* again, this time at the Palace, before taking it to New York, where he opened in it on Broadway in February 1958. That was the prelude to a burst of furious energy, mainly on films, but he did find time for two important returns to the stage—once in July 1959 to play once more the title-part in *Coriolanus*, this time at Stratford-on-Avon; and once in April 1960, in London, to play Berenger, the only character in Ionesco's *Rhinoceros* who contrived somehow to retain his human form. In the autumn of that year he went to America, dividing his time between Hollywood and Broadway; but in 1961 he was appointed Director of the newly-built Festival Theatre at Chichester, and came home to take up that post.

49. *Laurence Olivier in Herbert Wilcox's film of 'The Beggar's Opera'.*
50. *Olivier with Burt Lancaster in a film production of 'The Devil's Disciple'.*
51. *Olivier with Simone Signoret and Sarah Miles in Peter Glenville's film 'Term of Trial'.*

British Lion.

United Artists.

Warner-Pathé

52. Olivier with Marilyn Monroe in the film version of 'The Sleeping Prince', retitled 'The Prince and the Showgirl'.
53. Olivier with Kener Dullea and Anna Massey in Otto Preminger's film 'Bunny Lake is Missing'.
54. Olivier with Joan Plowright in Tony Richardson's film of 'The Entertainer'. *Warner-Pathé*

Columbia Pictures.

British Lion.

It was during this period that he married his third wife, Joan Plowright, who as a rising young actress had been in the cast òf *The Entertainer* at the Palace, and had since built up a considerable reputation for herself both in England and America. She and Olivier first acted together as husband and wife in the opening Chichester Festival, but neither then nor at any time since has it been correct, or even possible, to describe Joan Plowright as Laurence Olivier's leading lady. Ever since their professional association began they have been prominent members of the same repertory companies; but whether by accident or design, they have seldom been seen playing opposite one another in star parts.

Acceptance of the Chichester appointment was one of the characteristically brave gestures which mark Olivier's career. The theatre itself was an experiment, and everything about it was uncertain and unpredictable. The money for its building and endowment had been privately raised, Chichester itself had no theatrical tradition, there was no knowing whether a theatre in that part of the country would find a public, and even if it did, there was no knowing whether that public would approve of an open stage running out into the auditorium with seats on three sides of it.

If proof is needed of Olivier's dedication to the theatre in its artistic rather than its commercial aspect, it is surely here. Once before, for a patriotic motive, he had turned his back on an America which was offering him every inducement to stay; this time he was doing it again, but with no such over-riding compulsion behind him. He was doing it simply because the challenge of an artistic experiment interested him more than the acquisition of wealth.

His reward was the great satisfaction of carrying that first Chichester Festival to success on a scale for which its sponsors had not dared to hope. His choice of plays was in itself a display of courage: John Ford's tragedy *The Broken Heart,* John Fletcher's comedy *The Chances* and Chekhov's *Uncle Vanya.* The first two were half-forgotten pieces from the Jacobean era, revived presumably because they had been written for a platform stage and therefore would lend themselves to Chichester conditions. The third was selected, one can only suppose, because it had been a comparative failure at the Old Vic in 1944 and he wanted to go at it again; if so, he had an immediate satisfaction of seeing it the chief success of the Festival. He directed all three plays, but did not star himself as an actor. In *The Chances*, indeed, he did not appear at all, and in *Uncle Vanya* he took his old part of Astrov, the doctor.

Between the first and second Chichester Festivals he permitted himself a slight aberration, appearing in a second-rate suburban comedy called *Semi-Detached*. He had been much taken by the central character in this piece, an insurance-agent of dubious respectability; but the venture was not a success, and he returned to consideration of affairs at Chichester, which had now assumed a new importance. He knew by now that the long-looked-for National Theatre was shortly to come into being, and that he had been chosen to be its first artistic director; and naturally he began to look about him for the actors he would want with him in the company he would be called upon to form, some of whom were already with him at Chichester.

The appointment was made public in 1963, and the opening of the National Theatre—a great event in the history of the British stage no less than in Olivier's career—was announced for the autumn of that year at the Old Vic. The arrangement was that the Old Vic management should cease to function as such, and that its playhouse should become the home of the National Theatre for the time being, while its own more elaborate building was being designed, and approved, and constructed.

This was a complete reversal of the situation of 1949 when the Old Vic authorities, in the confident hope that they were going to be invited to merge into a national theatre, had arbitrarily relieved him of his directorship. There must have been a moment of personal satisfaction for Olivier when he inaugurated the rehearsals of *Hamlet* which, with Peter O'Toole in the name-part, was to be the National Theatre's opening production on 22nd October 1963.

However that may have been, he had reason for a wider satisfaction before long. Right from the start, the National Theatre caught the imagination of the play-going public. O'Toole's Hamlet won something less than the acclaim that had been hoped for it, but the *Uncle Vanya* production from Chichester, which by this time had become a notable example of team-acting, and

87

57. Laurence Olivier in the Chichester Festival production of 'The Broken Heart'.

58. Laurence Olivier with Maggie Smith in the National Theatre production of 'Othello'.

Angus McBean.

Angus McBean.

Farquhar's *The Recruiting Officer* both had complete success, as did *Saint Joan* and *Hobson's Choice,* in both of which Joan Plowright won great praise. The only complaints that were heard concerned the difficulty of obtaining seats. In this initial season Olivier contented himself, as an actor, with a modest contribution. He again appeared as Astrov in *Uncle Vanya,* and in *The Recruiting Officer* he took the small part of Captain Brazen.

During the first three seasons of the National Theatre he kept up his connection with Chichester, and once the National Theatre was launched and running on an even keel he used the Chichester Festivals of 1964 and 1965 to give preliminary trials to plays which he was considering for the Old Vic.

Once the new venture was safely under way, its director could find leisure (if that is the word) in which to do some large-scale acting himself. In April 1964 he gave that electrifying performance of Othello to which reference was made in the first section of this book, and followed it in June with Solness in *The Master Builder,* his wife for once playing opposite him as Hilda Wangel. In 1965 he directed *The Crucible,* and visited Berlin and Moscow with *Othello* and *Love for Love,* in which he played Tattle. This production was added to the Old Vic repertoire in October. In February 1967 he achieved one of his most startling disguises in Strindberg's *The Dance of Death.* At this point the doctors intervened. He was ordered to rest.

This enforced pause at the peak of Olivier's acting career must bring this brief survey of it to an end. It remains to attempt some answer to the question posed by the events of his life, namely what is his stature as an artist.

In one way, the answer is simple; in another, not. He has his detractors, like other eminent men; but there are few people who would attempt to deny his eminence, even his pre-eminence, among the English-speaking actors today. There was a time when a consensus of informed opinion might have awarded the palm to John Gielgud or Ralph Richardson, but it seems clear that that time has gone by. It is when we attempt to compare him with players of another age, or to make an assessment of his absolute quality that judgement becomes difficult.

An acute critic, Irving Wardle, has called Olivier the greatest performer within living memory. He is not a man to make unguarded decisions, yet surely this is a bold statement if it is fully realized that many people still alive can remember Henry Irving before his decline. Irving was the last of a race of giants, and Olivier has spent the whole of his strenuous career as a classic actor avoiding by every means in his power any touch of the gigantic.

From first to last, when Olivier played one of the great tragic roles, his aim was to find a new line on the character by scraping away accretions of theatrical tradition and making 'a real man' of him. In pursuit of this ideal he gave us a schoolboy Romeo, a Hamlet with a Freudian mother-fixation and a homosexual Iago. Having brought these characters down to earth, he would then play them with all the vigour, vitality and integrity which were his greatest assets. But in playing them so he forgot, or deliberately ignored, the basic fact that the heroes of classic tragedy, whether ancient Greek or Shakespearean, are not ordinary mortals. They are supermen, and to bring them down to earth inevitably robs them of dimension.

Backstage, where there is much serious discussion by actors of one another's methods and techniques, this slight limitation of Olivier's aims has by no means gone unnoticed. In *Letters from an Actor*, by the American William Redfield, there is an account of such a discussion, after which he gives his own firm assessment of Olivier. He first praises him for the strength of character which enabled him to refuse the blandishments of Hollywood in order to continue the stage career on which his heart was set, and then continues:

'Ironically enough, Laurence Olivier is less gifted than Marlon Brando. He is even less gifted than Richard Burton, Paul Scofield, Ralph Richardson and John Gielgud. But he is still the definitive actor of the twentieth century. Why? Because he wanted to be. His achievements are due to dedication, scholarship, practice, determination and courage. He is the bravest actor of our time.'

There is in this passage a clear observation that Olivier's approach to acting is different from that of his nearest rivals; but the statement that he is 'less gifted' than they are must be questioned because the writer has left out of his list of Olivier's virtues the one gift in which he most certainly surpasses them all—the essential gift which all truly great actors have had in common. This gift is creative energy, based on overflowing vitality.

It is this vitality which has given power to his temperamental urge to cut down the demigods, heroes and supermen of classic tragedy to human size. To impose this limitation on himself did of course make inevitable a certain lowering of aim, since poetic beauty was not to him, as it was to others, the supreme objective. Yet that very lowering of aim it was that made him 'the definitive actor of the twentieth century', for it gave him a target which he was able to hit again and again square in the middle, as a great actor should. The rest were left to touch greatness here and there in pursuit of an unattainable sublime.

59. Laurence Olivier with Joan Plowright in the National Theatre production of Ibsen's 'The Master Builder'.

Angus McBean.